Mastering Gypsy Oracle Cards

Advanced Guide to Interpreting the Sibilla della Zingara

M. Jacqueline Murray

COLE JACOBS BOOKS LLC

The information provided in this book, including any tips or recommendations, are meant to inspire the reader. The information provided is based on the author's experience and has been carefully considered prior to inclusion. Nevertheless, no guarantee can be granted nor is anything in this book a substitute for professional medical, psychological, legal or financial consultation. The author does not assume liability for the use or misuse of the information contained herein, nor for personal or material damage or financial losses.

Copyright © 2025 by M. Jacqueline Murray

All rights reserved. No part of this book may be used or reproduced in any form whatsoever without written permission except in the case of brief quotations in critical articles or reviews.

For more information, or to book an event, contact:
   http://www.geogypsyjacqui.com

Other books in the series by M. Jacqueline Murray:
   Gypsy Oracle Cards: A Handbook for Interpreting the Sibilla della Zingara

ISBN: 978-0-9991493-7-9 (Paperback)
ISBN: 978-0-9991493-8-6 (eBook)

First Edition: May 2025

For my devoted familiars, Aston and Martin,
keepers of secrets and chasers of spirits,
who see what others cannot.

**Other books in the series
by M. Jacqueline Murray:**

Gypsy Oracle Cards:
A Handbook for Interpreting
the Sibilla della Zingara

CONTENTS

**UNIQUE STRENGTHS OF
GYPSY ORACLE CARDS** 1

GYPSY ORACLE CARD ARCHETYPES 17
    2.1 Relationship Archetypes.. 24
    2.2 Emotion Archetypes 39
    2.3 Occupation Archetypes 53
    2.4 Events Archetypes 68
    2.5 Places and Things Archetypes 80
    2.6 States of Being Archetypes 92

INTERPRETING CARD COMBINATIONS 105
    3.1 Amplification 107
    3.2 Transformation 119
    3.3 Contradiction... 131
    3.4 Progression...145
    3.5 Balance 154
    3.6 Proximity and Influence 167
    3.7 Directional Energy 181

INTERPRETING REVERSED CARDS 197
    1. Internalized Expression 198
    2. Blocked or Obstructed Energy 198
    3. Shadow Aspects 199

    4. Developmental Challenges 199
    5. Compensatory Behaviour 200

ILLUSTRATIVE CROSS SPREAD INTERPRETATIONS 211
    Simple Cross Spread Interpretation 212
    Multi-layer Cross Spread Interpretation 242

QUICK REFERENCE GUIDES 249
    Upright and Reversed Card Meanings 249
    Table 1: Relationship Cards 249
    Table 2: Emotion Cards 252
    Table 3: Occupation Cards 254
    Table 4: Events Cards 256
    Table 5: Places and Things Cards 258
    Table 6: States of Being Cards 259
    Table 7: Positive Cards 261
    Table 8: Negative Cards 263
    Table 9: Neutral Cards 264
    Table 10: Amplification Combinations 265
    Table 11: Transformation Combinations 269
    Table 12: Contradicting Card Combinations 274
    Table 13: Comprehensive Progression Sequences 278
    Table 14: Comprehensive Balance Combinations 282

ABOUT THE AUTHOR 287

ACKNOWLEDGMENTS 289

CHAPTER 1

Unique Strengths of Gypsy Oracle Cards

Introduction

The Gypsy Oracle Cards, or Sibilla della Zingara, speak to us in a language that resonates with our deepest intuition. Unlike other divination systems, these cards have a remarkable way of bypassing the analytical mind and connecting directly with our inner wisdom. These cards don't just offer guidance; they awaken the intuitive voice that has always existed within us, waiting to be heard.

While this book offers structured methods and analytical techniques for card interpretation, I firmly believe that mastering these approaches isn't about memorizing rigid meanings. Rather, these techniques serve as bridges to your natural intuitive abilities. By learning these methods, you can bolster your intuition, enabling you to trust your insights when answering questions.

My personal journey with these cards has revealed six distinct strengths that make them unlike any other oracle system. I've found these qualities make the Sibilla both accessible for beginners and endlessly fascinating for those who've been reading cards for years.

1. Archetypal Organization: A Comprehensive Framework

Unlike other decks with their traditional suits and predetermined structures, I found the Sibilla has a more organic framework, one that encompasses all aspects of the human journey. Through careful observation and experience with countless readings, I noticed how these cards naturally group themselves into meaningful patterns that reflect different dimensions of human experience, and I developed a system to organize these cards into six natural archetypal categories that help to bring greater clarity and depth to interpretations.

Six Dimensions of Human Experience

The six categories; Relationship, Emotion, Occupation, Events, Places and Things, and States of Being, function as complementary lenses through which we can view any life situation. Together, they create a complete map of the human journey:

> **Relationship Archetypes**: Cards that reveal how human connections both empower and deplete us, showing the spectrum from nurturing support to challenging opposition.

Emotion Archetypes: Cards that illuminate the transient yet powerful emotional forces that colour our perception and drive our actions.

Occupation Archetypes: Cards representing forms of authority, expertise, and service that show how we position ourselves in hierarchies of influence.

Events Archetypes: Cards depicting pivotal moments and transitions that help us understand life as a sequence of meaningful changes.

Places and Things Archetypes: Cards representing environments and objects that show how physical spaces and possessions shape our sense of security and prosperity.

States of Being Archetypes: Cards embodying enduring modes of existence and persistent attitudes that colour our perceptions and shape our experiences.

Holistic Integration

What makes this categorization truly powerful is how it ensures that readings address all dimensions of experience. When cards from multiple categories appear in a spread, they naturally create a holistic picture that acknowledges the complex interplay between relationships, emotions, activities, events, environments, and internal states.

For example, a reading about a career change might include:

- **Occupation cards** revealing professional roles and expertise
- **Relationship cards** showing key connections affecting the transition
- **Emotion cards** illuminating feelings about the change
- **Events cards** indicating significant turning points in the process
- **Places and Things cards** suggesting material impacts and environments
- **States of Being cards** revealing persistent attitudes shaping the experience

This integrated approach provides a comprehensive understanding that other systems, which might emphasize one dimension over others, cannot match.

2. Narrative Clarity: The Art of Storytelling

Gypsy Oracle Cards are a valuable tool to empower the reader to construct clear, detailed narratives about specific life circumstances. While many divination systems offer symbolic insights that require significant interpretation, the Sibilla della Zingara tradition excels at telling straightforward stories that speak directly to practical concerns.

Direct Imagery and Meaning

The imagery of the Gypsy Oracle Cards employs people, objects, emotions, and situations that connect immediately to everyday experience. Unlike the more esoteric symbolism found in systems like Tarot, the Gypsy Oracle's visual language speaks in terms readily accessible to modern sensibilities.

Even though the images on the cards depict mid-19th century clothing and environs, cards like Journey, Wedding, or Conversation depict scenarios we can immediately recognize, making the system particularly suited for questions about practical matters and specific life situations. This accessibility allows readers to build narratives that resonate deeply with clients' situations, creating a sense of shared understanding and validation.

Sequential Development

The system's narrative power is further enhanced by its natural affinity for sequence and development. As explored in Chapter 3 under Progression, the cards reveal developmental sequences that tell cohesive stories with clear beginnings, middles, and endings.

For instance, the sequence "Conversation + Reunion + Wedding" depicts a progression from dialogue to reconciliation and, ultimately, formal commitment. The narrative's clarity allows readers to grasp not just individual points, but the overall development of the situation.

Character and Motivation

The inclusion of detailed relationship and emotion archetypes means that readings naturally address not just what happens but who is involved and how they feel. This creates stories with psychological depth that illuminate both external events and internal motivations.

For instance, a reading about workplace dynamics might reveal not just the presence of the Foe card indicating opposition, but also emotional cards like Haughtiness or Despair that explain the psychological drivers behind the conflict. This dimension adds richness to the narrative that purely situation-based readings might miss.

3. Psychological Depth: Beyond Practical Matters

Despite their practical focus and straightforward imagery, the Gypsy Oracle Cards access profound psychological patterns. They offer a bridge between pragmatic concerns and deeper psychological insights that make them uniquely valuable for personal development work.

Archetypal Psychology

Each card represents not just a situation or person, but an archetypal energy that resonates with universal human experiences. The cards tap into what Carl Jung called the collective unconscious, the patterns of experience that transcend individual circumstances and connect us to shared psychological realities.

For example, the Widower card goes beyond simply indicating loss or bereavement. It embodies the archetypal experience of profound grief and the psychological process of finding meaning through mourning. Similarly, the Prison card transcends literal confinement to represent the universal experience of limitation and the potential for transformation through constraint.

Shadow Integration

Challenging cards and reversed card interpretations naturally facilitate shadow work, helping users integrate unconscious or disowned parts of themselves. Cards like the Thief, Falseness, or Despair invite exploration of aspects of experience that might otherwise remain unacknowledged.

As explained in Chapter 4 on reversed cards, the system offers sophisticated approaches to reading challenging energies, whether through the shadow aspects, blocked energy, or compensatory behaviour interpretations. This psychological sophistication allows for readings that address both conscious intentions and unconscious patterns.

Emotional Intelligence

Readings frequently incorporate the emotional dimension of situations thanks to the availability of eleven emotion cards. This focus on emotional intelligence distinguishes the system from approaches that might emphasize external events or spiritual lessons without sufficient attention to emotional processing.

Cards like Melancholy, Sorrow, and Despair provide nuanced language for difficult emotional states, while Hope,

Joyfulness, and Cheerfulness illuminate different qualities of positive emotion. This emotional vocabulary creates space for authentic reflection on the full spectrum of human feeling.

4. Combinatory Richness: The Dance of Interaction

One of the most sophisticated aspects of the Gypsy Oracle tradition is its elaborate system for understanding how cards modify and interact with each other. The combinations of cards allow the reader to intuit a much broader spectrum of answers to the questions posed by seekers. When cards meet on the reading table, they create conversations far richer than their individual meanings could convey. With experience, readers recognize how card pairings create powerful resonances, or reveal transformative processes or tensions that mirror the complexity of human existence. This sophisticated web of card interactions distinguishes the depth of the Gypsy Oracle tradition from more simplistic divination systems.

Seven Principles of Combination

As detailed in Chapter 3, there are seven distinct ways that cards interact:

1. **Amplification** reveals how cards with complementary energies enhance and intensify each other. For example, Fortune alongside Money amplifies the prosperity message, creating "exceptional financial luck and abundant prosperity."

2. **Transformation** shows how one energy catalyzes change in another. Death followed by Child, for instance, reveals how "complete ending creates space for an entirely fresh beginning unburdened by the past."
3. **Contradiction** illuminates the tension between opposing energies. Wedding and Prison together expose "the fundamental tension between formal commitment and personal freedom."
4. **Progression** reveals developmental sequences and natural evolution. A sequence like Scholar + Doctor + Fortune shows how "learning and study leads to healing expertise, which ultimately creates prosperity."
5. **Balance** shows how complementary energies create equilibrium. Constancy paired with Frivolity suggests finding harmony between "steadfast dedication balanced with light-hearted spontaneity."
6. **Proximity** reveals how spatial relationships between cards create meaningful connections. Adjacent cards have stronger mutual influence than those farther apart, while geometric patterns form system relationships.
7. **Directional Energy** shows how cards influence each other through vectors of causality and flow. Journey flowing into Fortune suggests that "movement and change directly generate lucky circumstances."

This sophisticated framework for combination interpretation allows for readings of exceptional nuance and specificity, capturing the complex interplay of factors in any situation.

Beyond Simple Addition

Unlike systems where combinations are interpreted through simple addition or juxtaposition, the Gypsy Oracle tradition recognizes that card interactions create meanings that transcend what either card signifies alone. Simply put, new meanings emerge from the interplay of cards. For example, when Thought stands beside Journey, it creates a unique energy of "contemplative progress" that is distinct from either card's individual meaning.

This relational approach mirrors how complex systems function in real life, where outcomes emerge from the interaction of multiple factors rather than simple cause-and-effect relationships.

5. Balanced Perspective: Internal and External Realities

The Gypsy Oracle system achieves a remarkable balance between addressing external circumstances and internal states, material concerns, and emotional realities. This equilibrium makes it exceptionally versatile for exploring how objective situations and subjective experiences interrelate.

Bridging Inner and Outer Worlds

The six archetypal categories naturally span both external and internal dimensions:

- **External focus**: Events, Places and Things, and Occupation cards typically represent observable circumstances, material conditions, and social roles.
- **Internal focus**: Emotion and States of Being cards primarily illuminate subjective experiences, feelings, and attitudes.
- **Bridging both**: Relationship cards connect inner and outer experiences through the medium of interpersonal dynamics.

This balanced framework ensures that readings naturally address both what is happening externally and how it is experienced internally—a holistic perspective that many divination systems struggle to achieve.

Practical Spirituality

The Gypsy Oracle offers a unique bridge between everyday concerns and spiritual dimensions, what we might call "practical spirituality." Unlike systems that separate mundane matters from higher wisdom, these cards reveal how ordinary life experiences contain profound opportunities for spiritual lessons and psychological growth.

Each card operates simultaneously on multiple levels. The Money card, for instance, addresses immediate financial questions while revealing deeper patterns in how we create and experience abundance. The Wedding card speaks to literal partnerships while embodying the archetypal experience of sacred commitment that transforms individual identity through union with another.

This integration creates readings of immediate practical value that simultaneously illuminate the inquirer's spiritual journey. The cards reveal not just circumstances to be navigated, but how these experiences are shaping the inquirer's evolution, addressing both the outer path and the inner transformation occurring through life's challenges and blessings.

Material-Emotional Integration

Another powerful aspect of the Gypsy Oracle system is its revelation of the complex interplay between material circumstances and emotional states. Through the interaction of Places and Things cards with Emotion cards, readings expose the feedback loop where environments shape feelings and feelings create environments.

When House appears with Sorrow, for example, we see how physical spaces can contain or generate emotional heaviness, perhaps through memories embedded in a place, familial patterns connected to home, or physical surroundings that no longer support emotional wellbeing. Conversely, House with Joyfulness reveals how creating secure foundations enables authentic happiness to flourish.

These combinations help inquirers recognize how their external reality and internal landscape continuously shape each other, offering intervention points where changing either dimension can transform the whole system. This integration reveals that emotions are not merely subjective responses but creative forces that manifest in material form, while physical circumstances serve as containers that either nurture or challenge emotional development.

6. Developmental Insights: Evolution and Transformation

Where the Gypsy Oracle system truly distinguishes itself is in revealing how situations unfold through time. Beyond the static snapshots offered by many divination methods, these cards illuminate the dynamic processes of change that shape human experience, showing not merely what is, but how it came to be and what it is becoming.

Tracking Transformation

The cards naturally reveal transformational pathways through their interactions, showing the profound processes by which one state transmutes into another. This isn't merely about prediction, but about understanding the mechanisms of change itself.

When Misfortune transforms into Fortune, we witness the mysterious paradox where apparent disaster becomes the very catalyst for unexpected blessing and the collapse that creates space for new possibility. Similarly, the progression from Prison through Thought to Journey maps the liberation process: how confinement creates the conditions for necessary introspection that eventually enables authentic movement beyond limitation.

These transformational insights reveal life as a process rather than fixed circumstance, helping inquirers recognize themselves as participants in an unfolding story rather than victims of static conditions.

Life Cycle Awareness

The archetypal energies naturally organize into developmental sequences, mirroring life's organic rhythms. The progression from Child through Young Woman to Old Woman doesn't merely represent different people, but the maturation process within a single journey—from innocence through potentiality to embodied wisdom.

By recognizing these patterns, inquirers locate their current challenges within larger developmental cycles, gaining perspective that proves especially valuable during difficult transitions. What seems like an ending becomes part of a larger rebirth; what feels like confusion reveals itself as necessary reorientation.

Intervention Points

Perhaps most powerfully, the developmental nature of the cards reveals precise intervention points—those pivotal junctures where conscious action can most effectively redirect circumstantial flow. Rather than struggling against current conditions, inquirers learn to identify exactly where and how to apply their efforts for maximum effect.

When the cards reveal a progression from Falseness through Prison toward Death, for instance, the inquirer might recognize that their current experience of restriction (Prison) serves as necessary containment for processing deception before complete release can occur. Instead of fighting against limitation, they might work with this phase—using the enforced boundaries to gain clarity before moving toward completion and new beginning. This wisdom of timing transforms struggle into strategic participation with life's natural processes.

Conclusion: The Sibilla's Distinctive Wisdom

The Gypsy Oracle's six unique strengths create a system of exceptional versatility and depth. Through its comprehensive archetypal framework, narrative clarity, psychological depth, combinatory richness, balanced perspective, and developmental insights, the Sibilla offers a divination experience unlike any other.

What distinguishes these cards from other systems is not merely their individual meanings but the dynamic web of relationships they create a living, breathing ecosystem of archetypal energies that mirrors the complexity of human experience. The six archetypal categories ensure that readings naturally address all dimensions of life, while the seven principles of card combination create interpretations of remarkable nuance and specificity.

As you progress through this book, you'll encounter explorations of each card's meaning, learn sophisticated combination techniques, and develop a nuanced understanding of how cards interact within spreads. Each chapter builds upon the previous, creating a progressive journey into the heart of the Sibilla tradition. By integrating these lessons, what begins as intellectual understanding will gradually transform into intuitive knowing—the cards becoming not just objects you interpret, but voices you recognize.

The chapters ahead will equip you with practical techniques, developmental exercises, and interpretive frameworks that transform theoretical knowledge into embodied wisdom. Consistent practice with these methods will naturally improve your ability to sense subtle energies between cards, recognize developmental sequences intuitively, and understand how cards modify each other.

This book serves as your doorway into the profound tradition of the Gypsy Oracle; a tradition that offers not just divination but a complete language for understanding human experience in all its complexity. As you integrate these teachings, the cards will reveal themselves as not merely tools for prediction but as mirrors reflecting the dynamic, ever-evolving nature of life itself. Through this deepening relationship, you'll discover that the true magic of the Sibilla lies not in the cards themselves, but in the wisdom they awaken within you.

CHAPTER 2

Gypsy Oracle Card Archetypes

Introduction

During my years of working with the Gypsy Oracle Cards, I've developed a unique organizational system that reveals the natural archetypal patterns within the Sibilla della Zingara. What began as personal observations has evolved into a comprehensive framework that brings new clarity to this tradition. Rather than working with arbitrary classifications, I discovered that these cards naturally organize into six archetypal categories that together map the complete human experience.

This categorization emerged through practical application, noticing how certain cards consistently functioned in similar ways despite their varied imagery. Through my readings, I recognized distinct groupings that create a more coherent and insightful approach to interpretation. By organizing the cards according to these natural archetypes, readers can immediately identify which dimension of experience a card addresses, bringing greater precision to their readings.

The Six Archetypes of the Gypsy Oracle Deck

My framework comprises six fundamental categories that together encompass all aspects of human experience. Each category represents a distinct dimension through which we experience life, and together they create a complete map of the human journey.

1. Relationship Archetypes

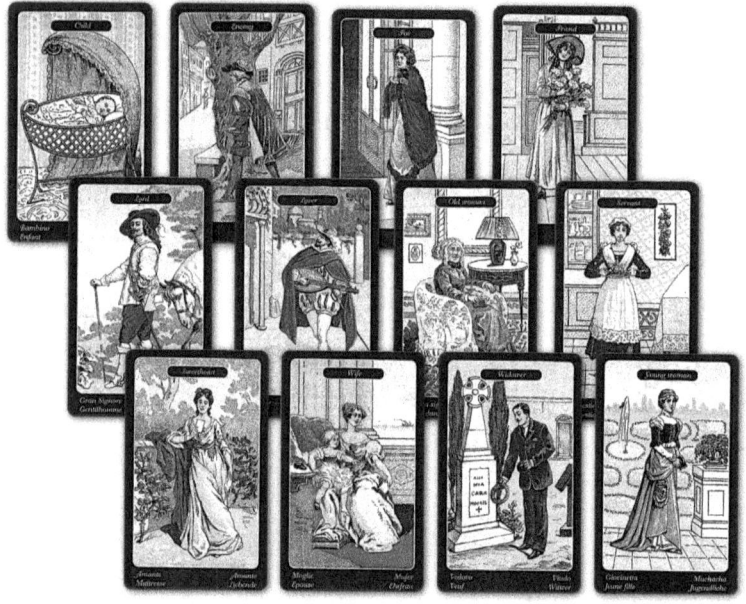

In my classification system, these cards illuminate the complex dynamics of human connections, showing both nurturing and challenging aspects of relationships. From Friend and Lover to Foe and Widower, these cards reveal how connections can support and empower us, but also how they can deplete and entangle us. They help us understand relationships as forces that shape our identity and facilitate growth.

2. Emotion Archetypes

These cards, which I've grouped based on their emotional qualities, unveil the subtle currents that shape our emotional reality. From Cheerfulness and Hope to Despair and Sorrow, they illuminate both the light and shadow aspects of our emotional landscape. They help us understand emotions as transient yet powerful forces that colour our perception and drive our actions.

3. Occupation Archetypes

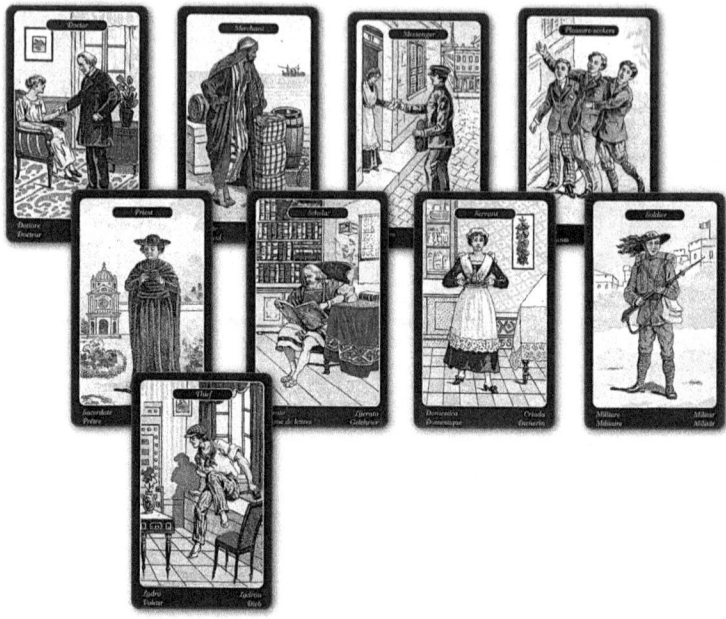

Occupation cards represent forms of authority, expertise, and service. Cards like Doctor, Merchant, Scholar, and Thief reveal how different professional roles and skills manifest in all aspects of life. Through studying their patterns in readings, I've discovered they show how we position ourselves in relation to others and navigate hierarchies of influence and responsibility.

4. Events Archetypes

Events cards represent significant occurrences, transitions, and turning points. From Journey and Wedding to Death and Misfortune, they illuminate the pivotal moments that shape our life journey. They help us understand life as a sequence of meaningful transitions rather than random occurrences.

5. Places and Things Archetypes

These cards represent the environments and material objects that structure our lives. Cards like House, Room, Prison, and Money reveal how physical spaces and possessions influence our sense of security, freedom, and prosperity. They show how we both shape and are shaped by our material reality.

6. States of Being Archetypes

These cards represent enduring modes of existence and persistent attitudes rather than temporary situations. They embody the ways we inhabit our lives from moment to moment, revealing our internal states and approaches to the world. Cards like Service, Waiting, Constancy, and Thought show how sustained conditions colour our perceptions and shape our experiences.

By understanding these six archetypal categories, readers can navigate the complex terrain of human experience with greater wisdom and clarity, offering guidance that honours the full complexity of life's journey.

Each archetype section provides a comprehensive understanding of the cards within that category. The sections begin with an overview of the archetype's significance, followed by a list of the specific cards belonging to that category. Next, each section explores the role these cards play in readings, explaining their energy dimensions and how they manifest in both supportive and challenging forms. Detailed synopses of each card are provided in both upright and reversed positions, offering nuanced interpretations of their meanings. Each section concludes with practical techniques for mastering interpretation of these cards, giving readers concrete tools to develop their intuitive understanding of the cards.

2.1 Relationship Archetypes

Relationship cards embody profound archetypal energies that illuminate the complex currents of human bonds, emotional attachments, and interpersonal dynamics. Each card serves as a window into the subtle energies that shape our interactions, revealing deeper truths about how we connect with others and navigate the intricate dance of human relationships.

Relationship Cards

Child	Enemy	Foe	Friend
Lord	Lover	Old Woman	Servant
Sweetheart	Wife	Widower	Young Woman

The Role of Relationship Cards in Readings

Relationship cards in a reading often signal a significant connection in the inquirer's life. Whether it's the supportive alliance of the Friend, the passionate attachment of the Lover, the wise counsel of the Old Woman, or the challenging opposition of the Foe, they reveal both the nurturing aspects of relationships that foster growth and the challenging dynamics that create opportunities for learning through difficulty.

The position of Relationship cards within a spread and their interaction with surrounding cards provides crucial insight into how these connections are manifesting in the inquirer's life. Are they in positions indicating recent influence, suggesting relationship patterns from the past are still active? Or do they appear in future positions, indicating developing connections that are yet to fully manifest? The position reveals much about the timing and evolution of significant relationships.

Particularly powerful insights emerge when multiple Relationship cards appear in a single reading, revealing the complex interplay of personal connections in the inquirer's life. The Friend alongside the Foe suggests supportive and challenging relationships simultaneously influencing a situation. The Young Woman near the Old Woman indicates the continuum of feminine energy from potential to wisdom affecting the inquirer's experience.

It's important to note that while many relationship cards in the Gypsy Oracle deck represent female archetypes (Young Woman, Old Woman, Wife, Sweetheart), this doesn't mean they only represent female persons in readings. Rather, these cards embody specific relationship energies or qualities that can manifest in any gender. The predominance of feminine symbols reflects the deck's historical context and its focus on the energetic qualities traditionally associated with different aspects of relationship dynamics. When interpreting these cards, focus on the archetypal energy they represent rather than restricting their meaning to a specific gender.

By developing sensitivity to the nuanced energies of Relationship cards, readers can help inquirers recognize the patterns in their connections with others, understand how these patterns relate to their inner landscape, and discover pathways toward more authentic and fulfilling relationships in all areas of life.

Most importantly, Relationship cards remind us that human connections are not simply external factors in our experience but profound forces that shape our identity, purpose, and growth. Through understanding the archetypal nature of relationships, inquirers can participate more consciously in creating connections that support their highest development while honouring the complex web of human interaction that gives life its deepest meaning.

Relationship Energy Dimensions

Each relationship card shows how personal bonds shape our experiences. These connections emerge through love, friendship, family ties, rivalry, and guidance. The cards also reveal how relationships can both support and challenge us, shaping our identity and growth.

Supportive Energies:

- Friend, Lover, Sweetheart, Lord: Support, devotion, and protection
- Wife, Old Woman, Servant: Nurturing, wisdom, and attentive care
- Child, Young Woman: Innocence and potential

Challenging Energies:

- Enemy, Foe: Active opposition and hidden betrayal
- Widower: Grief and endings

Card interactions reveal how relationships nurture or challenge us, create harmony or tension, and evolve through life stages. Chapter 3 discusses card interaction interpretations in more detail.

Relationship Cards Synopses

The following synopses, and those provided in subsequent sections, provide only a brief introduction to each card's meaning and interpretation within the Gypsy Oracle tradition. These concise descriptions highlight key aspects of the cards' archetypal energies but are not exhaustive. For a comprehensive exploration of each card, including detailed historical context, symbolic associations, and interpretation examples, readers should refer to my book "Gypsy Oracle Cards: A Handbook for Interpreting the Sibilla della Zingara." This more extensive resource offers in-depth guidance for both beginners and advanced practitioners seeking to master the rich symbolic language of this divination system.

Child

Represents innocence, new beginnings, and untainted potential. Shows how openness creates growth opportunities. Symbolizes strength found in vulnerability and starting anew without past conditioning.

In readings: Can literally mean pregnancy, birth, or childhood. May indicate new projects, relationships, fresh starts, or creativity. Suggests naïveté, inexperience, early stages, or needing to nurture something in order for it to flourish. Represents possibilities, beginnings, and creation.

Enemy

Represents opposition, confrontation, and forces working against you. Shows someone plotting or strategizing to undermine your personal or financial situation. Symbolizes unexpected obstacles that appear suddenly on your path.

In readings: A male rival or negative omen necessitates vigilance, careful information review, and a thorough situational assessment. Suggests someone plotting against the inquirer, blocking forward movement. The person may be motivated by perceived wrongs or revenge. The card suggests this opposition will appear unexpectedly, taking the inquirer by surprise. If followed by interruption cards, may indicate reconciliation or hostility ending.

Foe

Represents challenging energies, competition, and potential betrayal. Indicates deception, suggesting hidden threats that may not be immediately apparent. Symbolizes the need for vigilance and boundary-setting.

In readings: Can represent a female rival or signals interference in the inquirer's life from a person or event. Unlike the Enemy card, Foe represents someone visible to the inquirer, though possibly someone they trust. May indicate insincere friends, bad advice, or damaging gossip. The positive aspect is there's still time to avoid damage by recognizing the threat.

Friend

Represents supportive energy, faithful companionship, and trustworthy alliance. Embodies emotional support and genuine friendship, creating safety when navigating challenges. Symbolizes sanctuary in difficult times.

In readings: Indicates a person who provides friendship, aid, or good cheer. May be a counselor, confidante, or trustworthy supporter. Suggests a pleasant environment free of hostility with supportive people. Can announce favourable circumstances or events.

Lord

Represents mature masculine energy, protection, and noble intention. Provides guidance, structure, and support, showing how principled leadership creates safe environments.

Symbolizes honourable action, responsibility and a steadfast presence.

In readings: Can represent a successful man who is noble, well-meaning, kind, and trustworthy as a guide and protector. Suggests success, achievement, and fulfilment. With love cards, may indicate a destined partner. Can also represent employers, bosses, or important professional connections.

Lover

Represents romantic devotion, passionate attachment, and heartfelt adoration. Shows how open-hearted connection creates foundation for intimate partnership. Symbolizes transformative potential of romantic love.

In readings: Almost always positive for love questions. Typically represents a devoted partner, honest, generous, sweet, and sincere. For male inquirers, likely represents them. Can symbolize falling in love, promising improvements in various aspects of life.

Old Woman

Represents feminine wisdom, experience, and intuitive knowledge. Shows how accumulated experience provides perspective during challenges. Symbolizes patience, perspective, and traditional values.

In readings: As a persona, this card represents a senior family member, matriarch, or grandmother. Can represent a wise woman who gives good advice, suggesting the inquirer should trust counsel from an older woman. May represent advice from experience, wisdom, or intuition from someone trusted, or the inquirer's inner voice. In marriage contexts, could refer to mother-in-law or mother. Can also represent a peaceful, traditional family environment.

Servant

Represents supportive care, attentive help, and selfless contribution. Shows how attentiveness to needs creates value. Symbolizes both the strength and potential vulnerability in service roles.

In readings: Indicates someone loyal, respectful, and helpful who provides service or collaboration. Suggests service provided in a friendly, hospitable way that creates comfort. Shows someone nearby who cares for the inquirer. Also warns that service is provided for compensation, suggesting caution about surrounding oneself with people who might serve for personal gain rather than sincere intentions.

Sweetheart

Represents feminine romantic energy, emotional depth, and receptivity. Shows how emotional openness creates authentic intimacy. Symbolizes the intersection of passion and tenderness.

In readings: For female inquirers, represents them as a person in love, suggesting positive answers to love questions. Indicates a sweet and charming relationship period, mutual love and affection. Can represent any loving female, friend, wife, girlfriend, or sister. With other love cards, may predict engagement or wedding.

Wife

Represents nurturing feminine energy, commitment, and domestic harmony. Shows how consistent care creates stability and belonging. Symbolizes committed female energy, creating sustaining emotional environments.

In readings: Represents someone generous, intellectual, confident, thoughtful, morally sound, trustworthy and dependable. For inquirers hoping to be a wife, suggests this wish will come true, or finding an ideal partner to build a life with. In business, represents someone who helps implement projects and supports success.

Widower

Represents profound loss, grief, and emotional processing. Shows how acknowledging completion is essential for transition and renewal. Symbolizes finding meaning through mourning that eventually leads to new understanding.

In readings: Represents feelings associated with significant loss or separation - whether the end of a relationship, job loss, business failure, or actual bereavement. Indicates sadness, loneliness, and regret that can feel overwhelming. Can represent someone who hasn't moved past a loss. Warns that we often don't appreciate what we have until it's gone.

Young Woman

Represents emerging feminine energy, potential, and development. Shows how openness creates pathways for growth. Symbolizes the beginning stages of feminine wisdom with all the potential while maintaining flexibility.

In readings: Can represent a good, sensible young female or a situation needing to grow/mature. Can indicate youthful enthusiasm, new ventures not yet producing results. With negative cards, may suggest being restrained, confined, or forced to mature too quickly.

Reversed Relationship Cards Synopses

Reversed Child

Indicates compromised innocence or interrupted development. Suggests childishness rather than childlike qualities. Represents the wounded inner child needing healing. Warns of exploited vulnerability or resistance to new beginnings.

Reversed Enemy

Indicates the end of an argument, hostility, or obstacle. Can suggest that a deception was merely a joke or a close call. May indicate that danger was detected or an enemy disarmed before damage occurred. When accompanied by negative cards, could suggest a resolved problem might be reactivated.

Reversed Foe

Indicates enemies becoming allies or conflicts losing intensity. Suggests possible misidentification of threats or internalized opposition where the real conflict is within. May indicate transformation of rivalry into productive competition.

Reversed Friend

Indicates compromised trust or unreliable support. Points to one-sided relationships creating resentment or dependency. Represents superficial connections masking as genuine friendship. Warns of possible betrayal or lack of support when needed. May suggest difficulty receiving help or trusting others.

Reversed Lord

Indicates distorted masculine energy where protection becomes control or strength becomes domination. Suggests authority figures who abuse their position or fail in their role. Represents shadow aspects of masculine energy through aggression or irresponsibility. Warns of father figures who disappoint or betray trust.

Reversed Lover

Suggests unrequited affection, emotional immaturity, or inability to form deep connections. Represents partnerships where passion has dimmed, needing emotional renewal. Warns of codependent attachments masquerading as love. May indicate need to develop self-love first.

Reversed Old Woman

Indicates rigidity or bias rather than wisdom. Suggests outdated perspectives that no longer serve present circumstances. Represents manipulation or excessive caution. Warns of clinging to the past or rejecting valuable traditional knowledge.

Reversed Servant

Suggests betrayal of trust or an employee who takes advantage, is unproductive, or lazy. Shows someone working against the inquirer rather than providing support and help. May indicate inquirer's inability or unwillingness to accept help or practice self-care. Almost always signals uncomfortable situations or difficult times when help is unavailable.

Reversed Sweetheart

Indicates distorted or manipulative feminine romantic energy. Suggests insincerity or defensive barriers to authentic connection. Warns against using emotional appeal as control. May indicate unrequited affection or investment in unavailable partners.

Reversed Wife

Indicates resentment or martyrdom, distorting nurturing energy. Suggests domestic disharmony or mechanical rather than heartfelt care. Represents shadow aspects of commitment expressing through control or manipulation. Warns of excessive self-sacrifice creating imbalance.

Reversed Widower

Indicates either incomplete grief processing or completed mourning. Suggests inability to acknowledge losses, creating unresolved grief. Represents potential for new beginnings, moving forward after mourning. Warns against becoming defined by loss rather than transformed through it.

Reversed Young Woman

Indicates suppressed feminine potential or inappropriate development. Suggests immaturity or arrested emotional development. Represents premature responsibilities before psychological readiness. Warns of naivety creating vulnerability to exploitation.

Practice Techniques for Mastering Interpretation of Relationship Cards

When relationship cards emerge in a reading, they invite deeper exploration that transcends literal interpretation. As a reader, you can move beyond surface meanings to uncover the complex relational energies that shape the inquirer's connections and reveal pathways for more fulfilling and authentic relationships.

To help you develop your intuition for interpretation of the cards, the following sections present question lists for common relationship questions.

Relationship Quality Exploration

- What type of connection does this card suggest?
- How deep or meaningful is the relationship indicated?
- What stage of development is this relationship experiencing?
- What qualities characterize this connection?
- How stable or volatile is this connection?

Emotional Landscape Inquiry

- What emotions are associated with this relationship?
- How do these emotions influence the overall situation?
- What unspoken feelings might be present beneath the surface?
- How is emotional energy exchanged in this relationship?
- What emotional needs are being met or neglected?
- What emotional patterns tend to repeat in this connection?

Power Dynamics Analysis

- Who holds influence or authority in this relationship?
- How is power being used or misused within the connection?
- What might need rebalancing for healthier interaction?
- How are decisions made within this relationship?
- What boundaries need to be established or maintained?

Transformational Potential Questions

- How might this relationship evolve over time?
- How might this relationship support personal growth?

- What lessons are being offered through this connection?
- What potential for positive change exists within this bond?
- What patterns from the past might be healed through this relationship?

Trust and Authenticity Considerations

- How genuine is this relationship?
- What level of trust exists between the parties?
- Are there hidden agendas or undisclosed motivations?
- How openly are thoughts and feelings shared?
- What barriers to authenticity exist in this connection?

2.2 Emotion Archetypes

Emotion cards represent archetypal energies illuminating the complex landscape of human experience. Each card reveals subtle currents shaping emotional reality and deeper truths about our inner world.

Emotion Cards

Cheerfulness	Despair	Faithfulness	Falseness
Haughtiness	Hope	Joyfulness	Love
Melancholy	Sorrow	Surprise	

The Role of Emotion Cards in Readings

Emotion cards serve as windows into the inner landscape of the inquirer, revealing the subtle currents and complex patterns that shape their emotional experience. Rather than simply indicating fleeting feelings, these cards illuminate the deeper archetypal energies that influence how we perceive, process, and respond to life's circumstances.

When emotion cards appear in a reading, they often highlight the particular emotional qualities or challenges active in the situation, whether it's the celebratory joy of Cheerfulness, the faithful constancy of Faithfulness, the reflective sadness of Melancholy, or the intense vulnerability of Despair. They reveal both the constructive potential of these emotions when processed consciously and the shadow aspects that emerge when feelings remain unconscious or unintegrated.

The position of emotion cards within a spread and their relationship to surrounding cards provides crucial insight into how these emotional energies are manifesting in the inquirer's life. Are they in positions suggesting current experience, revealing what's being felt in the present moment? Are they in future positions, indicating emotional states that are developing? Or do they appear in positions related to past influences, showing the emotional patterns that have shaped current circumstances?

Particularly powerful insights emerge when multiple emotion cards appear in a single reading, revealing the complex emotional landscape the inquirer is navigating. Cheerfulness paired with Melancholy suggests a bittersweet experience. Hope alongside Despair indicates the tension between optimism and fear. Love in connection with Sorrow points to the deep grief that can accompany profound attachment.

By developing sensitivity to the nuanced energies of emotion cards, readers can help inquirers recognize which feelings they need to acknowledge, which emotional patterns they need to transform, and which emotional qualities they need to cultivate. In this way, emotion cards serve not just as indicators of current feelings but as guides to emotional intelligence, helping inquirers develop greater emotional awareness, balance, and authenticity as they navigate life's complex emotional terrain.

Emotional Energy Dimensions

Each card represents a unique emotional state shaping experiences and potential. The archetypal energies reveal how feelings can both inspire and connect, but also overwhelm and isolate.

Positive Emotional Energies:

- Cheerfulness, Joyfulness: Celebratory energy that connects and uplifts
- Hope, Faithfulness: Forward-looking emotions that sustain and support
- Love, Surprise: Transformative emotions that open and expand the heart

Challenging Emotional Energies:

- Despair, Sorrow: Overwhelming emotions revealing deepest vulnerabilities
- Falseness, Haughtiness: Deceptive emotions masking authentic experience
- Melancholy: Reflective emotion processing pain into wisdom

Emotion Card Synopses

Cheerfulness

Represents celebratory energy, social joy, and exuberant happiness. Creates moments of communal delight and triumph. Symbolizes uniting people on joyous occasions.

In readings: Favourable energy, signalling auspicious occasions, social events, receptions, weddings, celebrations. May suggest getting out more or enjoying yourself. Indicates good mood affecting all aspects of life. Brings light and enthusiasm to any situation.

Despair

Represents darkest emotional depths, jealousy, and overwhelming negative feelings. Reveals deepest vulnerabilities and fears. Symbolizes the need for emotional awareness and control.

In readings: A negative card revealing confusion and unreasonable thoughts from despair, desperate jealousy, envy, lost love, and sorrow. Warns of dangers when emotions like humiliation, resentment, self-pity, or intense envy take control, potentially leading to destructive behaviours or isolation.

Faithfulness

Represents loyalty, trust, reliability, and emotional constancy. Maintains emotional bonds through challenges. Symbolizes the transformative potential of trust and faith.

In readings: A positive card symbolizing loyalty, fidelity, and faithfulness. Suggests the inquirer can count on support from friends, family, and colleagues. Indicates protection and encourages trusting instincts. With love cards, suggests relationships built on solid foundations of trust and loyalty.

Falseness

Represents deception, insincerity, and misleading appearances. Reveals gaps between appearance and reality. Symbolizes the power of truth-seeking and the need for authenticity.

In readings: A negative card suggesting caution and watchfulness, as flattery may conceal cheating and falsehoods. Indicates betrayal, deception, lies, corruption, and defensiveness. May represent something fake, a two-faced person, or efforts to cover mistakes or lies. Warns that things may not be as they seem and cautions against false flattery or double dealing.

Haughtiness

Represents pride, self-importance, and excessive self-regard. Shows how ego can both empower and isolate. Symbolizes strength found in balanced self-esteem.

In readings: Communicates an attitude of superiority, pride, or lack of humility. Indicates arrogance, conceit, vanity, showing off, or excessive ambition. Warns against becoming excessively proud, though a healthy ego is good. With many positive cards, can indicate something to be proud of—an achievement or success approaching.

Hope

Represents inner vision, optimistic anticipation, and faith in positive outcomes. Sees beyond immediate circumstances, providing emotional sustenance during difficult times. Symbolizes the power of belief in possibilities.

In readings: A positive card encouraging that relief for current situations is coming. Suggests anticipation and belief in a positive outcome. Indicates ability to see possibilities where others see only obstacles. Suggests maintaining faith during challenges helps both the inquirer and those around them. Hope works best paired with action.

Joyfulness

Represents heartfelt happiness, genuine delight, and emotional fulfilment. Creates deep, authentic, positive emotional experiences beyond superficial pleasures. Symbolizes purest form of positive emotional energy.

In readings: A very positive card signifying joy, lightheartedness, and merriment. Indicates glee, gaiety, and pleasure from entertainment or creativity. Suggests satisfaction, relief, resolution, and celebration, often connected to achievements or promotions. Signals a period of joy and happiness, assuring wishes will be satisfied.

Love

Represents the most powerful emotional connection, passion, and deep affection. Creates profound bonds and emotional openness between people. Symbolizes ultimate emotional fulfilment.

In readings: A positive card symbolizing love and eroticism. Indicates a new love is born or happiness in love. Represents affection, intense feelings, romance, and sensuality. A very positive omen for love life, suggesting no impediments. For existing lovers, an invitation to awaken love and improve it.

Melancholy

Represents reflective sadness, contemplative grief, and emotional processing. Finds meaning through emotional challenges. Symbolizes the potential of properly processed sadness.

In readings: Represents sadness, resignation, and suffering with dignity. Suggests dwelling on mistakes and disappointments, feelings of abandonment, depression, upset, grief, anxiety, and regrets. Refers to preoccupation with past regrets, mistakes, losses, or disappointments. Implores gathering energies to move beyond these feelings rather than remaining stuck.

Sorrow

Represents acute grief, intense emotional pain, and profound loss. Reveals depth of attachments through their loss. Symbolizes the journey through emotional pain.

In readings: Symbolizes sorrow and loss. Indicates profound sadness, anguish, pain, and grief, often related to separation, heartbreak, or serious problems with money or health. Suggests experiencing deep grief related to circumstances—perhaps significant losses or ended stability. By honouring this sorrow rather than suppressing it, creates a foundation for genuine recovery.

Surprise

Represents unexpected joy, fortunate discoveries, and positive revelations. Brings sudden shifts in emotional states. Symbolizes the transformative quality of unexpected blessings.

In readings: Represents surprise, unexpected joy, or positive events. Indicates unexpected money, rewards, wins, bonuses, or surprise visits, letters, or calls. Brings unexpected developments to situations, highlighting serendipity, better than expected outcomes, pleasant discoveries that weren't planned.

Reversed Emotion Card Synopses

Reversed Cheerfulness

Indicates negative response to inquiry, denied job, failed exam, unsuccessful pregnancy, or more serious events like interrupted wedding, broken engagement, illness, or death. Suggests betrayals, lies, enemy presence, and obstacles, with general malaise, laziness crisis, lack of enthusiasm, or lost trust. With many positive cards, could represent social situation discomfort or forced revelry without true joy.

Reversed Despair

Suggests extreme emotional distress is interrupted. Continues overwhelming feelings but urges considering causes and advises against impulsive or inappropriate actions. May signal end to reckless or irrational behaviours. Confusion, disorder, nervousness are possible. Urges continuing life with courage, tackling problems possibly with loved ones' help.

Reversed Faithfulness

Indicates inconsistency, hesitation, impulsive behaviour, and instability. May represent an unfair or unreliable friend. Suggests lack of commitment causing dissatisfaction. In love matters, shows lack of commitment, fidelity, or dedication. At work, inconsistency leads to missed opportunities. In relationships, suggests weak foundations requiring caution.

Reversed Falseness

Indicates end of falsehood, truth emerging, secrets revealed, and deceptions uncovered. Insincere behaviours, gossip, slander, jealousy, and envy will cease. May answer the inquirer's question, indicating no deceit. With negative cards, could suggest worse-than-anticipated situations involving betrayals, affairs, or infidelity from partners, employees, family, and friends.

Reversed Haughtiness

Suggests a healthy awareness of limitations and strengths. May indicate needing more self-assurance and pride. Can indicate resuming friendships or relationships, or improving dealings with colleagues with whom you've been competing. Mainly indicates resolved past behaviour rather than strongly influencing surrounding cards.

Reversed Hope

Suggests disrupted future plans. Warns that hopes for the situation at hand are misplaced. Enthusiasm will dampen or expectations dashed. Represents pessimistic mood or discontent with situation outcomes. Only when associated with rival or enemy cards could this positively message ending others' hopes to take advantage of or defeat the inquirer.

Reversed Joyfulness

Indicates real disappointment. Warns of approaching difficult times with doubt and uncertainty. Times ahead may bring sadness, disappointments, broken friendships, or financial challenges. In work situations, indicates concern; in family relationships, disagreement and disharmony. Only with "interruption" cards does it signify ending "dark" periods and approaching happiness.

Reversed Love

Suggests love ending or unrequited love. Portends volatility, infidelity, love and marriage frustration, lost love, falling out of love, lost attraction, or sexual incompatibility. Warns that the other person offers nothing, expecting no love, tenderness, or affection. Signals loneliness or sadness periods. Only with very strong positive cards could it imply ending loveless periods.

Reversed Melancholy

Only positive when associated with ending cards, suggesting end of melancholy periods. Otherwise more negative, suggesting emotional breakdown, failed love, unhappy family situation, or friendship, job, or money loss. Association with love or wedding cards reinforces negative interpretation as irreversible break, impossible situation, mourning, divorce, or separation.

Reversed Sorrow

Can be positive, representing healing. Suggests ending periods of confusion, sickness, hindrance, or emotional suffering. Represents moving beyond grief into healing. In relationships, implies parties can resolve issues like misunderstandings, conflicts, or obstacles. For physical ailment inquiries, suggests ending convalescence periods.

Reversed Surprise

Advises wanted or needed messages or information are not coming. Signifies negative or "no" answers. May result from messenger inaction rather than inquirer actions. Suggests events or developments not happening as expected or being delayed. If waiting for love interest expressions, they won't come soon, if at all. Conversely, for bad news waiting, indicates it's not coming.

Practice Techniques for Mastering Interpretation of Emotion Cards

When Emotion cards emerge in a reading, they invite deeper exploration that transcends literal interpretation. As a reader, you can move beyond surface meanings to uncover the complex emotional energies that shape the inquirer's inner landscape and reveal pathways for more authentic emotional expression.

To help you develop your intuition for interpretation of the cards, the following sections present question lists for common emotional themes.

Emotional Quality Exploration

- What is the primary emotional energy present in this situation?
- How deeply is this emotion influencing the circumstances?
- Is this emotion appropriate to the situation or disproportionate?

- What emotional needs are being expressed or suppressed?
- How conscious is the person of their emotional state?

Emotional Pattern Inquiry

- Is this a recurring emotional theme for the inquirer?
- What triggers this particular emotional response?
- How does this emotion connect to past experiences?
- How has this emotion evolved over time?
- How does this emotion interact with other feelings?

Emotional Balance Analysis

- Is this emotion in healthy proportion or excessive?
- How is this emotional energy affecting decision-making?
- What complementary emotion might bring greater balance?
- What emotional resources are available for regulation?
- How might emotional intelligence be applied here?
- What would emotional maturity look like in this situation?

Transformational Potential Questions

- How might this emotion serve as a catalyst for growth?

- What wisdom or lesson is embedded in this emotional experience?
- How can this emotion be channeled constructively?
- How might emotional awareness transform this situation?
- What gifts lie hidden within this emotional state?

Authenticity and Expression Considerations

- How genuinely is this emotion being experienced or expressed?
- Are there hidden or denied emotions beneath the surface?
- What healthy outlets exist for this emotional energy?
- How might authentic emotional expression change the situation?
- How does culture influence emotional expression here?
- What would complete emotional authenticity reveal?

2.3 Occupation Archetypes

Occupation cards represent archetypal energies illuminating human authority, expertise, and service. Each card provides insight into interactions, power structures, and human intention, showing how different forms of expertise manifest in all aspects of life.

Occupation Cards

Doctor	Merchant	Messenger	Pleasure	Seekers
Priest	Scholar	Servant	Soldier	Thief

The Role of Occupation Cards in Readings

When occupation cards appear in a reading, they often highlight the particular form of expertise or authority needed in the situation, whether it's the diagnostic precision of the Doctor, the strategic acumen of the Merchant, the protective discipline of the Soldier, or the communicative clarity of the Messenger.

Beyond simply representing literal professions or career paths, these cards illuminate the deeper currents of how we exercise power, share knowledge, and navigate the complex terrain of human hierarchies. They reveal both the constructive potential of these energies when expressed in balanced ways and the shadow aspects that emerge when these powers are misused or underdeveloped.

The position of occupation cards within a spread and their relationship to surrounding cards provides crucial insight into how these archetypal energies are manifesting in the inquirer's life. Are they in positions of strength, suggesting skills and authorities that can be consciously wielded? Or do they appear reversed or in challenging positions, revealing areas where expertise is blocked or authority is being misapplied?

Particularly powerful insights emerge when multiple occupation cards appear in a single reading, revealing the interplay of different forms of expertise and authority. The Doctor paired with the Scholar suggests healing through knowledge. The Merchant alongside the Messenger indicates prosperity through strategic communication. The Priest in connection with the Servant points to spiritual growth through humble service.

By developing sensitivity to the nuanced energies of occupation cards, readers can help inquirers recognize which forms of expertise they need to develop, which authorities they need to question, and which services they need to offer or receive. In this way, occupation cards serve not just as descriptors of external roles but as guides to internal development, helping inquirers cultivate the full spectrum of archetypal powers available to them as they navigate life's complex journey.

Authority and Expertise Energy Dimensions

Each card represents a unique manifestation of authority and expertise, showing how professional roles shape human interactions and potential. These cards demonstrate that power emerges through knowledge, service, protection, and strategic maneuvering.

Positive Occupation Energies:

- Doctor, Scholar, Priest: Healing and transformative power of knowledge and wisdom
- Merchant, Messenger: Strategic exchanges creating value and connection
- Soldier, Servant: Protection and support maintaining order and providing care
- Pleasure Seekers: Liberating power of collective emotional expression

Challenging Occupation Energies:

- Thief: Shadow side of expertise—manipulation and exploitation of vulnerabilities
- Reversed Doctor: Misuse of healing authority for personal gain or control
- Reversed Soldier: Protection becoming oppression, discipline becoming rigidity
- Reversed Priest: Spiritual authority distorted by dogma or moral hypocrisy

Occupation Card Synopses

Doctor

Represents healing authority, medical wisdom, and power to diagnose and remedy. Understands complex systems and restores balance in physical bodies, emotional states, or life situations. Symbolizes transforming pain into healing.

In readings: Usually positive, indicating crisis resolution. When representing a person, suggests informed and assured advice, wise guidance, comfort, and authoritative direction. Indicates need to resolve situations, abandon unproductive paths, or emerge from stagnation. With positive cards, suggests favourable events and helpful people.

Merchant

Represents economic authority, strategic negotiation, and value creation. Masters exchange, recognizing potential and opportunity where others see barriers. Symbolizes creating prosperity through intelligent interaction.

In readings: A good omen for business and trade, suggesting affirmative answers to success questions. Symbolizes business skills, successful commerce, and financial success. May represent a successful competitor in business, selling, negotiation, or investing, a leader with foresight and good instincts. Rarely negative unless with challenging cards, where it suggests greed, cunning, stinginess, or scheming.

Messenger

Represents expertise in communication, information transfer, and connection across boundaries. Knows what to communicate and when and how to deliver for maximum impact. Symbolizes the potential of knowledge and timing.

In readings: Usually positive, signalling arrival of important information or documents. May arrive via various media and from distant places or people. With "love" cards, suggests attention to communication, including non-verbal signals between partners. For work or career, usually signals good news unless associated with negative cards. Emphasizes importance of both message and timing.

Pleasure Seekers

Represents expertise in emotional expression and social dynamics. Shows power of spontaneity and collective energy. Symbolizes the transformative potential of unrestrained experience.

In readings: Interpretation heavily depends on adjacent cards and inquiry nature. With positive cards, can indicate fun but disorderly gatherings. With negative cards, represents crazy thoughts, agitation, recklessness, or delirium. May suggest being swept up in crowds or negatively influenced by peers. Warns of potential confusion, misunderstandings, or impulsive behavior leading to regret.

Priest

Represents spiritual authority, moral judgment, and institutional wisdom. Interprets universal laws and ethical frameworks. Symbolizes intersection of personal conscience and collective belief systems.

In readings: A neutral card symbolizing the sacred, higher power, and universal laws defining good versus evil. May suggest examining one's conscience and remind of personal responsibility for thoughts and actions. Serves as a reminder that life extends beyond the physical world. Thematically suggests pressing legal matters requiring attention. Rarely refers to specific people unless other cards indicate this.

Scholar

Represents intellectual authority, deep contemplation, and transformative knowledge. Analyzes, synthesizes, and understands complex information, discerning hidden patterns and truths. Symbolizes wisdom transcending immediate circumstances.

In readings: Usually represents a well-educated, trusted advisor. A person of culture, knowledge, and status who can be trusted for wisdom, wise counsel, and discretion. This person knows facts, is well-informed, or can identify core issues. Generally calm, sensitive, serious, and values silence over excessive talking. Relies on reason rather than physical strength, offering measured guidance based on careful consideration.

Servant

Represents expertise through supportive service, anticipatory care, and selfless contribution. Intuitively understands and responds to others' needs before explicitly requested. Symbolizes strength found in humble, dedicated service.

In readings: Suggests someone loyal, respectful, and helpful, providing service or collaboration in a friendly, comfortable manner. Indicates someone nearby who cares for the inquirer. Warns that service is provided for compensation, suggesting caution to surround oneself with sincere people, not those serving only for personal gain.

Soldier

Represents institutional authority, protective energy, and disciplined action. Excels in maintaining boundaries, strategic planning, and precise execution. Symbolizes structured approach and unwavering commitment.

In readings: Interpretation heavily influenced by situation and associated cards. Often represents a person in authority, soldier, police officer, or similar. When not representing an individual, embodies suspicion, jealousy, mistrust, protectiveness, or defensiveness. May signify justice or law enforcement. In business, it might indicate faithful partners or trustworthy employees. With positive cards, suggests protection, serious commitment, and practical support.

Thief

Represents expertise in understanding systemic vulnerabilities and hidden pathways. Recognizes concealed opportunities and alternative routes others miss. Symbolizes adaptability and unconventional problem-solving.

In readings: A negative card suggesting sudden or unexpected property loss, love, time, or work. Warns that superficiality or inattention allows falling prey to ill intentions. Represents wickedness, bad intentions, misdeeds, and harmful thoughts that rob possessions, confidence, good faith, or security. Frequently suggests dishonest people will take advantage when guards are down. With negative cards, suggests significant loss, robbery, scam, or fraud.

Reversed Occupation Card Synopses

Reversed Doctor

Suggests misdiagnosis or improper assessment, indicating fundamental flaws in problem analysis or approaches. Points to codependency disguised as helping, where supposed healers perpetuate problems to maintain rescuer roles. Warns of potential exploitation under guise of assistance. Suggests overidentification with helper roles, stagnating personal growth and creating imbalanced relationships.

Reversed Merchant

Indicates exploitation or purely transactional relationship approaches, calculating every interaction for maximum personal gain without concern for mutual benefit. Suggests financial losses, poor business judgment, or failed negotiations from shortsightedness or ethical compromises. Represents valuing material gain over meaningful values. Warns of potential unethical business practices sacrificing integrity for profit.

Reversed Messenger

Indicates miscommunication, gossip, or distorted messages. Suggests important information that is blocked, delayed, or misinterpreted. Represents failure to bridge gaps or connect different perspectives. Warns of potential rumour spreading or unclear communication creating confusion rather than connection. Suggests inability to deliver difficult communications or avoiding uncomfortable truths.

Reversed Pleasure Seekers

Indicates hedonism, addiction, or escapism, where pleasure becomes compulsion and celebration transforms into avoidance. Suggests inability to find joy, resulting in either numbing withdrawal or pursuing increasingly extreme sensations. Warns of potential peer pressure overriding individual judgment. Suggests lack of emotional boundaries, emotional manipulation or exploitation of others' desires.

Reversed Priest

Indicates moral hypocrisy, judgment, or ethical rigidity, using spiritual principles as control weapons rather than guidance tools. Suggests spiritual bypass or using religion/morality to avoid emotional work. Represents spiritual authority misuse or manipulation through guilt, shame, or fear serving ego rather than spiritual values. Warns of potential dogmatism reducing complex ethical questions to simplistic formulas.

Reversed Scholar

Represents intellectual arrogance or knowledge misuse as a weapon or shield rather than understanding tool. Indicates analysis paralysis preventing action. Suggests a disconnect between theory and practical application. Warns of potential information manipulation or spread of misinformation. Represents blocked learning or resistance to new ideas, turning existing knowledge into dogma preventing growth.

Reversed Servant

Indicates martyrdom, self-sacrifice, or enabling behaviour, where service becomes self-negation rather than purposeful assistance. Suggests servility, lack of boundaries, or people-pleasing tendencies undermining authentic relationships. Represents resentment from unreciprocated giving. Warns of potential codependency or unhealthy helping patterns. Suggests inability to recognize or address personal needs due to identity wrapped in serving others.

Reversed Soldier

Indicates excessive rigidity, control, or authoritarian behaviour, where protection becomes oppression and discipline becomes punishment. Suggests aggression, bullying, or protective power misuse to dominate rather than defend. Represents undisciplined action or inability to maintain appropriate boundaries. Warns of potential blind obedience to undeserving authorities. May also suggest defensiveness preventing vulnerability or connection.

Reversed Thief

Indicates victimization or being taken advantage of, becoming the target rather than the perpetrator of exploitation. Suggests unconscious self-sabotage or self-theft, unknowingly robbing oneself of opportunities through self-defeating behaviour. Represents wasted resources through neglect, mismanagement, or poor boundaries. Warns of potential dishonesty compromising integrity and self-respect. May indicate blind spots regarding personal vulnerabilities. When associated with positive cards may indicate near miss or interrupted theft.

Practice Techniques for Mastering Interpretation of Occupation Cards

When Occupation cards emerge in a reading, they invite deeper exploration that transcends literal professional interpretation. As a reader, you can move beyond surface meanings to uncover the complex energetic patterns of authority, expertise, and service that shape the inquirer's relationships and approach to life's challenges.

To help you develop your intuition for interpretation of the cards, the following sections present question lists for common occupational themes.

Professional Credibility Exploration

- How does the person relate to authority figures in this situation?
- What specific qualities suggest trustworthiness or expertise?
- Are there indications of genuine skill or potential deception?

- How might the professional role be masking underlying intentions?
- What unspoken credentials or hidden qualifications might be at play?
- What expectations exist around professional boundaries?

Motivational Landscape Inquiry

- What deeper desires might be driving the current situation?
- What unacknowledged needs are being expressed through this archetype?
- How do personal ambitions intersect with professional responsibilities?
- What hidden agendas might be subtly influencing the interaction?

Power Dynamics Analysis

- Who holds the true power in this situation?
- How are control and influence being negotiated?
- What unspoken hierarchies are being established?
- Are there potential power imbalances that need careful navigation?
- How might traditional power structures be challenged or reinforced?
- Where does vulnerability exist within the power dynamic?
- How is authority being established or undermined?

Transformational Potential Questions

- How can the current situation be leveraged for meaningful change?
- How might this archetype facilitate personal evolution?
- What limitations need to be transcended?
- What skills or perspectives are being called forth?
- What patterns must be broken for transformation to occur?
- What aspects of self are emerging through this experience?

Ethical and Systemic Considerations

- What moral boundaries are being tested?
- How do personal ethics interact with professional expectations?
- Are there systemic constraints limiting potential?
- What unwritten rules are influencing the situation?
- How might integrity be maintained or compromised?
- What responsibilities exist toward various stakeholders?
- How do cultural or societal values impact this situation?

2.4 Events Archetypes

In Gypsy Oracle Cards, Events cards represent archetypal energies illuminating pivotal moments, transitions, and encounters shaping our life journeys. They reveal dynamic forces moving us forward, connecting us with others, transforming circumstances, and marking significant passages.

Events Cards

Conversation	Death	Fortune	Journey
Malady	Misfortune	Reunion	Wedding

The Role of Events Cards in Readings

When Events cards appear in a reading, they often signify there's a transition currently unfolding, whether it's the forward movement of Journey, the reconnection of Reunion, the definitive closure of Death, or the fortunate turning point of Fortune. They reveal both the constructive potential of transitions when embraced consciously and the challenges that emerge when we resist necessary change.

The position of Events cards within a spread and their relationship to surrounding cards provides crucial insight into how these transitional energies are manifesting in the inquirer's life. Are they in positions indicating recent influence, suggesting transitions already underway? Or do they appear in future positions, indicating developments yet to unfold? The position reveals much about the timing and development of significant events.

Additional insights emerge when multiple Events cards appear in a single reading, revealing the sequence or progression of transitions occurring in the inquirer's life. Journey followed by Conversation suggests movement leading to important dialogue. Death preceding Child indicates complete ending making space for a new beginning. Reunion leading to Wedding shows reconciliation developing into formal commitment.

By developing sensitivity to the nuanced energies of Events cards, readers can help inquirers recognize which transitions are currently shaping their experience, how these changes connect to past developments, and what future possibilities they might create. In this way, Events cards serve not just as indicators of external occurrences, but as maps of the meaningful transitions that create the narrative arc of our lives.

Most importantly, Events cards remind us that life is never static, it flows continuously through cycles of beginning and ending, connection and separation, fortune and challenge. By understanding the archetypal nature of significant events, inquirers can participate more consciously in their unfolding story, finding meaning and purpose in even the most difficult transitions.

Event Energy Dimensions

Each Event card represents a unique manifestation of transitional or transformative energy. These pivotal moments emerge through movement, connection, celebration, challenge, and change. They reveal both constructive and challenging aspects of significant moments and show us how events can precipitate growth opportunities but also disrupt and destabilize.

Positive Event Energies:

- Journey, Conversation: Dynamic energies of movement and connection
- Reunion, Wedding: Harmonizing energies of coming together and commitment
- Fortune: Transformative energy of fortunate circumstances and timing

Challenging Event Energies:

- Death, Misfortune: Disruptive energies forcing radical transformation
- Malady: Destabilizing energy requiring healing
- Reversed Journey: Frustrating energy of blocked progress or detour

Events Cards Synopses

Conversation

Represents dialogue, idea exchange, clarification, and social connection. Encourages meaningful communication and shared understanding. Symbolizes the need for clear expression and open hearing.

In readings: A positive card indicating favourable moments regarding life, friendships, and relationships. Foreshadows meetings or gatherings with important information exchange, or opportunities for clarification, explanations, or apologies. Indicates the inquirer will be heard in discussions. With love cards, suggests intimate dialogue; with negative cards, may indicate hindered communication. For business meetings or job interviews, generally indicates positive outcomes.

Death

Represents profound ending, irrevocable transformation, and necessary release. Brings closure to completed cycles and facilitates attachment release. Symbolizes the power of definitive transition and rebirth.

In readings: Almost always means something ending. Should not be feared, as endings make way for transformation in natural universal cycles. Suggests something will be irreversibly lost—love, job, trip, business, career, or happy times—potentially resulting in something better. Indicates need for profound, radical change, possibly difficult but necessary. May signal sudden painful events leading to anguish, despair, violence, trauma, or weakness, marking stormy periods possibly shifting to more positive developments later.

Fortune

Represents luck, unexpected favour, abundance, and positive fate turns. Suggests fortuitous circumstances or chance events bringing emotional or monetary windfalls. Symbolizes the unpredictable nature of beneficial circumstances.

In readings: A very positive card regarding wealth or well-being, regardless of inquiry. Weakens negative cards like failure, death, or ending, suggesting interruption of negative situations as fate intervenes for the inquirer. Can indicate sudden inheritance, win, or chance meeting. It invariably casts a positive light on any situation.

Journey

Represents movement, progress, travel, and life transitions. Embodies dynamic power of forward momentum and exploration. Symbolizes profound capacity to evolve through movement.

In readings: A positive change for the inquirer. Most literally means location change, travel (business or pleasure), or someone coming or going. Often indicates long-distance travel. Beyond physical movement, can represent evolving situations moving forward or resolving. While mostly positive, can sometimes indicate saying goodbye to someone or something moving away.

Malady

Represents illness, weakness, vulnerable states, and necessary recovery. Identifies systemic imbalance and dysfunction. Symbolizes the need for a period of rest and recuperation.

In readings: Suggests something "sick" causing suffering requiring time before recovery. Could also represent loneliness from isolation or confinement. Indicates temporarily weakened states requiring proper diagnosis, care, and recovery time, whether in health, relationships, work, or other life areas.

Misfortune

Represents catastrophic setback, devastating loss, and profound challenge. Shows how sudden reversals can completely alter paths and self-understanding. Symbolizes a transformative crisis forcing complete rebuilding.

In readings: A negative card suggesting accidents, failures, or serious problems changing things for the worse. Can indicate love loss, job loss, business venture failure, or grave-consequence errors. Almost always suggests lost causes or unrecoverable/irreparable losses, potentially including foreclosure, debt, or deep relationship rifts. Warns little can be done to prevent or mitigate situations, leaving inquirers to deal alone. With very positive cards, might signal necessary complete destruction to start again with new foundations, suggesting something wonderful may emerge from ashes.

Reunion

Represents reconnection, reconciliation, and coming together after separation. Heals divisions and reestablishes broken connections. Symbolizes the potential of forgiveness and restoration.

In readings: Indicates encounters or meetings resulting in clarification, resolution, or fresh starts. Between separated lovers, signals positive reconciliation and beloved's return. Can represent meetings between friends, family or business associates to resolve conflicts, begin new projects, or resume partnerships. Suggests possible invitations to such meetings or the need for important discussions to move forward.

Wedding

Represents pivotal moments of formal commitment, union, contract, and public declaration. Shows how relationships gain strength through formalization and community acknowledgment. Symbolizes the positive potential of partnership and commitment.

In readings: A positive card representing partnership, marriage, engagement, responsible love, the materialization of hope, signed agreement, contract realization, or significant new beginnings. Contains elements of authority, law, or destiny in the union. In love matters, indicates true, sincere, approved, and requited love. In other situations, represents significant meetings or partnerships being forged, indicating formal commitments bringing structure and public recognition to important relationships or agreements.

Reversed Events Cards Synopses

Reversed Conversation

Indicates communication breakdown where messages become distorted or missed. It suggests postponed discussions that allow issues to fester, one-sided exchanges without genuine listening, and potentially harmful gossip. At its core, it represents the inability to express what truly matters due to fear or pride, creating emotional distance instead of connection.

Reversed Death

Indicates resistance to necessary endings, creating prolonged suffering through attachment to what should be released. Suggests situations stuck in painful limbo, neither completed nor able to renew. Represents fear of letting go that blocks potential new beginnings. Shows transformative processes that have stalled midway, requiring conscious effort to complete the necessary release and rebirth.

Reversed Fortune

Indicates delayed or diminished luck where expected positive outcomes fail to fully materialize. Suggests temporary setbacks before eventual good fortune - the darkness before dawn. Represents missed opportunities or benefits arriving when no longer needed. Warns of illusory "fool's gold" that lacks substance upon closer examination or taking existing good fortune for granted.

Reversed Journey

Suggests blocked progress where momentum is impeded by external obstacles or internal resistance. Indicates delayed travel plans or relocations keeping one stationary despite desires to move. Shows apparent movement without actual advancement. Warns of detours or wrong directions. Reveals reluctance to embrace necessary transitions due to fear of leaving the familiar.

Reversed Malady

Indicates recovery from illness or weakness, with healing processes successfully restoring strength. Suggests the end of confinement periods, representing liberation from restrictive circumstances. Shows returning vitality after depletion, demonstrating resilience when properly supported. Indicates addressing root causes rather than just symptoms. Reveals wisdom gained through vulnerability that remains valuable as strength returns.

Reversed Misfortune

Indicates recovery from disaster or prevention of anticipated calamity. Suggests valuable learning through challenges that ultimately strengthen rather than destroy. Shows discovery of unexpected blessings within apparent catastrophe. Represents resilience and capacity to weather seemingly overwhelming storms. Indicates "near misses" that provide important warnings without delivering the full impact.

Reversed Reunion

Suggests missed connections where anticipated reconciliations don't materialize as expected. Indicates cancelled meetings that delay potential resolution. Shows gatherings that occur physically but not emotionally. Warns of reconciliations based on illusion rather than genuine resolution. Suggests premature reuniting before necessary individual growth has occurred, perpetuating patterns rather than creating renewal.

Reversed Wedding

Indicates commitments that fail to materialize or formalize. Suggests agreements with hidden complications creating future difficulties. Represents premature commitment before establishing true compatibility. Warns of feeling trapped by formal arrangements that once seemed desirable. Shows partnerships where public declaration masks private ambivalence, creating gaps between appearance and reality that undermine stability.

Practice Techniques for Mastering Interpretation of Events Cards

When Events cards emerge in a reading, they invite deeper exploration that transcends literal interpretation. As a reader, you can move beyond surface meanings to uncover the complex transitional energies that shape the inquirer's journey and reveal pathways for more conscious participation in life's pivotal moments.

To help you develop your intuition for interpretation of the cards, the following sections present question lists for common transitional situations.

Event Nature Exploration

- What type of occurrence or transition does this card suggest?
- How significant or far-reaching is the event indicated?
- What phase or stage of this event is currently unfolding?

- Is this event primarily internal or external in nature?
- How disruptive or harmonious is this transition likely to be?
- How will this occurrence impact different life domains?

Timing and Sequence Inquiry

- When might this event occur or be occurring?
- What preceded this event and what might follow?
- How does this event fit into larger patterns or cycles?
- Is timing crucial to how this event unfolds?
- What preparatory steps might be beneficial?
- How quickly or slowly should this transition proceed?
- What natural rhythm or timing is at work here?

Agency and Influence Analysis

- How much control does the inquirer have over this event?
- What forces are influencing how this event unfolds?
- How might the inquirer best navigate this occurrence?
- What aspects can be directed versus what must be accepted?
- Who else has significant influence over this situation?

- What cosmic or karmic forces might be at work?

Transformational Potential Questions

- How might this event serve as a catalyst for growth?
- What wisdom or lesson is embedded in this experience?
- What potential for positive change exists within this occurrence?
- How might this transition reveal hidden aspects of self?
- What new capacities might emerge through this experience?
- What limitations might be transcended through this event?

Impact and Consequence Considerations

- Who will be most affected by this event?
- What immediate and long-term impacts might this event create?
- How might this transition affect relationships?
- What resources might be gained or lost?
- How might this event change one's direction or priorities?
- What unseen benefits or challenges might emerge?

2.5 Places and Things Archetypes

Places and Things cards represent far more than mere physical locations or objects. They embody profound archetypal energies that illuminate the settings, containers, and exchanges that shape our human experience. Each card serves as a window into the symbolic environments and meaningful objects that structure our lives, revealing deeper truths about how we create, inhabit, and navigate our material and psychological worlds.

Places and Things Cards

Gift	House	Letter
Money	Prison	Room

The Role of Places and Things Cards in Readings

When Places and Things cards appear in a reading, they highlight the particular environmental qualities or challenges active in the situation, whether it's the protective stability of House, the intimate privacy of Room, the confining restriction of Prison, the resourceful abundance of Money, the unexpected blessing of Gift, or the intentional communication of Letter. They reveal both the constructive potential of these environments when consciously engaged and the shadow aspects that emerge when our relationship with spaces and objects remains unconscious.

The position of Places and Things cards within a spread and their relationship to surrounding cards provides crucial insight into how these environmental energies are manifesting in the inquirer's life. Are they in positions suggesting current experience, revealing the spaces and objects currently influencing the situation? Are they in future positions, indicating environmental shifts that are developing? Or do they appear in positions related to past influences, showing the material patterns that have shaped current circumstances?

When multiple Places and Things cards appear in a single reading, they unveil the complex environmental landscape the inquirer is navigating. House paired with Prison suggests the tension between security and confinement. Money alongside Gift indicates the interplay between earned and unearned abundance. Letter in connection with Room points to the delicate balance between communication and privacy.

By developing sensitivity to the nuanced energies of Places and Things cards, readers can help inquirers recognize which environments support their development, which material patterns they need to transform, and which physical or symbolic spaces they need to create. In this way, Places and Things cards serve not just as indicators of current surroundings but as guides to environmental intelligence, helping inquirers develop greater awareness of how they both shape and are shaped by the material world they inhabit.

Environmental and Material Energy Dimensions

Each card represents a unique manifestation of environmental or material energy. These cards show how physical spaces and objects shape our experiences through security, connection, restriction, abundance, and communication.

Supportive Environmental Energies:

- House, Room: Protective energies of security and personal space
- Money, Gift: Abundant energies of resources and unexpected blessings
- Letter: Connecting energy of communication across distance

Challenging Environmental Energies:

- Prison: Confining energy limiting movement and choice
- Reversed House: Destabilizing energy of domestic dysfunction
- Reversed Money: Restrictive energy of scarcity and insecurity

Places and Things Cards Synopses

Gift

Represents generosity, offerings, unexpected blessings, and recognition. Creates bonds through meaningful offerings.

Symbolizes strength found in generosity and acknowledgment.

In readings: A good omen suggesting the realization of aspirations or arrival of gifts or inheritance. Indicates winnings, abundance, situation improvement, successful endeavours, achievement, or flattery. Suggests situations dramatically improving after uncertainty or helpful interventions. Represents overcoming obstacles leading to success and esteem.

House

Represents security, stability, family foundation, and domestic harmony. Creates spaces of protection, belonging, and rootedness. Symbolizes capacity to provide sanctuary and continuity.

In readings: A positive card symbolizing either a physical place (home, epicentre) or feelings of security, solidity, and prosperity. Represents family bonds, home, office, security, responsibility, self-reliance, and independence. Suggests a stable environment with family harmony, representing the essence of the situation.

Letter

Represents communication, information, written exchange, and documentation. Bridges distances through recorded messages. Symbolizes the power of personal communication and record-keeping.

In readings: A neutral card signifying communication or news that could be positive or negative, usually personal in nature. Indicates messages, answers, approvals, contracts, documents, or new opportunities/challenges. Specifically refers to written communications, both physical and digital.

Money

Represents material wealth, resources, value, and exchange. Reveals relationship with abundance and scarcity. Symbolizes the power of financial freedom and choice.

In readings: A positive card symbolizing money, abundance, and good fortune. Indicates inheritance, winnings, luck, with success and prosperity within reach. Suggests confidence, self-worth, and success. Considered a positive omen of financial well-being from family, winnings, or business. Reminds of the importance of saving for changing fortunes and budgeting appropriately.

Prison

Represents confinement, restriction, punishment, and forced introspection. Exposes limitations and consequences of actions. Symbolizes transformative potential of confronting confines.

In readings: A negative card symbolizing mental or physical confinement. Implies difficulty moving on, shame, guilt, self-punishment, anxiety, regret, remorse, exile, or loneliness. Most commonly represents something locked, closed, or inability to break free. Suggests temporary conditions allowing for reflection on mistakes.

Room

Represents privacy, introspection, intimacy, and personal space. Creates boundaries and interior retreats. Symbolizes the need for focused attention and private contemplation.

In readings: A neutral card representing a private tranquil place for gathering thoughts or intimate meetings. Indicates intimacy, privacy, receiving guests, being welcomed, or a need to retreat and reflect. Describes a tranquil, orderly atmosphere suggesting reflection or confidential encounters.

Reversed Places and Things Cards Synopses

Reversed Gift

Represents loss—gifts not received, lost inheritance, or unexpected debt. Can indicate inability to save, squandered money, financial market losses, sales of items for money, or bad investments. With "Thief" card, may indicate theft, scams, or blackmail.

Reversed House

Very negative, symbolizing breakdowns in family relationships, quarrels, misunderstandings, or broken dreams. For relationship questions, signifies breakups, broken engagements, divorce, or dissolved partnerships. Warns to evaluate relationships in all contexts—home, office, friends. May signal the end of business relationships or enterprise failures.

Reversed Letter

Suggests expected letters, documents, or information won't arrive or will be late. Could be a loved one not writing as promised, missing confirmations, or withheld invitations. Doesn't indicate bad or good news, just that expected communication won't arrive as anticipated. May suggest the inquirer has failed to reach out to someone waiting for them.

Reversed Money

Signals money loss through gambling, waste, or vain spending. Only positive when associated with "ending" cards signalling the end of stagnation, poverty, misery, or financial hardship. Usually warns of complications from inadequate funding due to overspending, squandered inheritance, depleted savings, or poor investments.

Reversed Prison

Suggests the punishment term has ended. May still represent negative situations, but indicates release from confining circumstances. Closed-mindedness, prejudice, negative thoughts, regrets, and remorse are possible restraints being lifted. Most positively interpreted as freedom from negative situations.

Reversed Room

Signifies a world turned upside down—inner turmoil, confusion, loss of perspective. Indicates impulsive behaviour, inability to manage situations before they deteriorate or to restore order. Suggests complex, tangled situations full of obstacles and complicated relationships. May indicate material loss of home, office, or property.

Practice Techniques for Mastering Interpretation of Places and Things Cards

When Places and Things cards emerge in a reading, they invite deeper exploration that transcends literal interpretation. As a reader, you can move beyond surface meanings to uncover the complex environmental energies that shape the inquirer's surroundings and reveal pathways for more intentional engagement with spaces and objects.

To help you develop your intuition for interpretation of the cards, the following sections present question lists for common environmental questions.

Environmental Nature Exploration

- What environment or object does this card suggest?
- How significant is this environment to the inquirer's situation?
- Is this space or object temporary or more permanent?
- What qualities characterize this environment or object?

- What unspoken dynamics exist within this environment?
- How permeable or fixed are the boundaries of this space?

Material Relationship Inquiry

- What relationship does the inquirer have with this environment or object?
- How does this space or item influence the overall situation?
- What unacknowledged patterns might be present in this environment?
- How do resources flow through this space or object?
- What material needs are being met or neglected?
- How might environmental awareness transform this situation?

Boundary Dynamics Analysis

- What defines the limits of this space or object?
- How are boundaries being maintained or crossed?
- What might need rebalancing for healthier environmental interaction?
- What containment issues are occurring beneath the surface?
- How are decisions made about this environment?
- What boundaries need to be established or dissolved?
- How might appropriate containment be fostered?

Transformational Potential Questions

- What lessons are being offered through this environment or object?
- How might this environment evolve over time?
- What potential for positive change exists within this setting?
- What qualities need development to improve this environment?
- What patterns from the past might be healed through this space?
- What new possibilities might emerge through this environment or object?

Authenticity and Alignment Considerations

- How authentic is this environment to the inquirer's true needs?
- What level of congruence exists between the space and its purpose?
- Are there hidden functions or purposes of this environment or object?
- How clearly are boundaries defined?
- How might greater environmental integrity transform this situation?

2.6 States of Being Archetypes

States of Being cards represent the profound archetypal energies that illuminate the essential modes of existence, internal attitudes, and persistent ways of engaging with the world. Each card serves as a window into the enduring states that colour our perceptions, guide our actions, and shape our experiences, revealing deeper truths about how we inhabit our lives from moment to moment.

States of Being Cards

| Consolation | Constancy | Frivolity | Service |
| Sighs | Thought | Waiting | |

The Role of States of Being Cards in Readings

When States of Being cards appear in a reading, they often highlight the particular persistent conditions or attitudes active in the situation, whether it's the patient anticipation of Waiting, the unwavering dedication of Constancy, the reflective consideration of Thought, or the wistful longing of Sighs. They reveal both the constructive potential of these states when engaged consciously and the limiting aspects that emerge when these modes become rigid or unconscious.

The position of States of Being cards within a spread and their relationship to surrounding cards provides crucial insight into how these persistent conditions are manifesting in the inquirer's life. Are they in positions suggesting current experience, revealing the habitual ways of being that dominate the present moment? Are they in future positions, indicating modes of existence that are developing? Or do they appear in positions related to past influences, showing the enduring states that have shaped current circumstances?

When multiple States of Being cards appear in a single reading, allow the reader to access the complex internal landscape the inquirer is navigating. Service paired with Sighs suggests the tension between helping others and attending to personal yearnings. Constancy alongside Frivolity indicates the challenge of balancing reliability with spontaneity. Thought in connection with Consolation points to the integration of analytical reflection and emotional comfort.

By developing sensitivity to the nuanced energies of States of Being cards, readers can help inquirers recognize which persistent conditions serve them, which habitual modes limit them, and which states they need to cultivate. In this way, States of Being cards serve not just as indicators of current conditions but as guides to conscious living, helping inquirers develop greater awareness, balance, and intentionality as they navigate life's complex terrain.

States of Being Energy Dimensions

Each States of Being card represents a unique manifestation of sustained condition or mode of existence, revealing how these persistent states shape our experiences and potential. These cards demonstrate that our ongoing states are multifaceted, emerging through various channels of service, anticipation, consistency, thought, comfort, lightness, and longing.

The archetypal energies of states of being reveal the fundamental ways we inhabit our lives over time. They illuminate both the constructive and challenging aspects of persistent conditions—how certain states can create stability and fulfilment, but also how they can create stagnation and limitation.

Supportive State Energies:

- Service, Constancy: The grounding energies of helpfulness and reliability
- Thought, Consolation: The stabilizing energies of reflection and comfort
- Waiting: The focused energy of patient anticipation

Challenging State Energies:

- Frivolity: The ungrounded energy of excessive lightness
- Sighs: The wistful energy of unfulfilled longing
- Reversed Service: The depleting energy of self-sacrifice without boundaries

The interaction between states of being cards can reveal our complex internal landscape—how certain attitudes reinforce or counterbalance others, how persistent states evolve over time, and how our habitual ways of being shape our experience of life's events and relationships.

States of Being Cards Synopses

Consolation

Illustrates comfort, relief, solace, and easing of difficulty. This archetype represents the power of support during challenging times. Symbolizes the transformative potential of timely comfort, embodying both receiving and giving of comfort and support.

In readings: A very positive card that predicts doubts and worries will give way. The card suggests realization of desires, satisfaction, unexpected opportunity, a favourable period, and positive changes, results, and events. It may also indicate approval, honours, or recognition that comes unexpectedly.

Constancy

Personifies steadfastness, reliability, and unwavering commitment, with expertise in maintaining consistent effort and devotion. This archetype represents dependable presence and steady application, symbolizing the transformative potential of persistent dedication in both literal consistency and psychological steadiness.

In readings: A positive card assuring that commitment and determination overcome life's difficulties. It indicates reliability, consistency, and solidity, suggesting a purposeful, prudent, patient person focused on long-term endeavours. May also represent lack of change, accountability, or fixed circumstances.

Frivolity

Represents lightness, playfulness, and carefree attitude without seriousness. This archetype embodies the liberating power of treating matters lightly, bringing lightness to situations while symbolizing both the positive and negative aspects of not taking things seriously.

In readings: Generally positive, suggesting lightness and a carefree existence, though it indicates superficial, often irresponsible behaviour of someone who jumps between activities, underestimating situations' gravity. Warns of perilous behaviour potentially causing later regrets from unconsidered actions.

Service

Represents helpful action, support, assistance, and dutiful attention. Embodies the nurturing power of serving others or causes through practical aid and responsive support, symbolizing the profound capacity to attend to needs, representing both literal work and helpful attitude.

In readings: A positive card indicating help is available. Shows receiving or offering assistance respectfully and dutifully. May represent someone providing service from loyalty and care or from self-interest. Can also indicate the inquirer's own work or services provided.

Sighs

Illustrates longing, yearning, wistfulness, and emotional expectation. Represents the power of desire and anticipation by revealing deep yearnings and unspoken wishes, symbolizing the transformative potential of acknowledged desire between hope and uncertainty.

In readings: Depicts emotions, thoughts, and anxieties while awaiting an answer or following rejection. Shows searching for solutions with anticipation. May indicate isolation, abandonment, loneliness, or separation states.

Thought

Represents contemplation, reflection, analysis, and mental deliberation. Expertly examines ideas and processes information, symbolizing the power of careful consideration and reasoned judgment through both active thinking and meditative reflection.

In readings: A neutral card representing the need for reflection and addressing inner struggles. Suggests taking time to think before making decisions. Can represent an insight from reflection or a thoughtful person who considers carefully before deciding.

Waiting

Embodies anticipation, expectation, patience, and suspended action. Masters remaining alert during passing time by maintaining focus during inaction, symbolizing the tension between present moment and future development.

In readings: A positive card symbolizing anticipation for someone or something to arrive. Suggests yearning, hoping, or wanderlust, indicating the future arrival of a person, news, or opportunity after a necessary waiting period, with ultimately positive outcomes.

Reversed States of Being Cards Synopses

Reversed Consolation

When this card is reversed, it signifies missed or wasted opportunities. Literally, the failure to receive consolation suggests that the failure is due to forces external to the consultant, a fluke rather than a consequence. It could suggest a lack of comfort or an unexpected disappointment.

Reversed Constancy

When reversed, this card indicates inconsistency, hesitation, impulsive behaviour, and lack of stability. It may also represent an unfair or unreliable friend. It can suggest a lack of commitment will result in dissatisfaction. In matters of love, there could be a lack of commitment, fidelity, or dedication. At work, inconsistency will lead to missed opportunities. With respect to relationships, this card reversed can suggest there is a lack of firmness or foundation to a relationship.

Reversed Frivolity

This card is considered positive when it appears reversed. It could spell the end of superficial or irresponsible behaviour. It takes on a negative meaning only if it signals the end of a carefree time. This card is strongly influenced by other cards. If associated cards suggest a past painful event, reversed this card suggests it will be some time before cares will be lifted.

Reversed Service

When reversed, this card suggests that not only will help not arrive, but it warns of someone who undermines the inquirer's efforts, a rival in the workplace, or a loved one that is working at crossed purposes. It can also suggest the presence of someone who appears to be helpful but is, in reality, harmful. It warns of the presence of someone two-faced, an unfaithful friend, a dishonest employee, or someone who is disloyal.

Reversed Sighs

Reversed, this card indicates the end of a time of waiting for something desired. The "sighs" for something or someone are over. The associated cards are necessary to give clarification. The anxiety may have passed because the desired person has returned, a wish has been granted, or a dream has come true. Conversely, it could mean that there is no hope, that feelings of love are unrequited, or a dream has vanished.

Reversed Thought

When this card appears reversed, it suggests lack of thought, consideration, or reflection, or a person that acts in a thoughtless, impulsive way. This could suggest that the inquirer has not given a situation or decision enough thought or has given in to desires and passions without thinking through the consequences. This card is a warning to review what you are doing, to stop and think. It can also suggest a troubled mind, worry, or anxiety that is not productive.

Reversed Waiting

This card reversed represents waiting unnecessarily, or disillusionment. As this card is an indicator of time, reversed it is a suggestion to stop waiting, that it is pointless or all hope is in vain. It suggests that an event will not occur or a person will not come. This could be that a loved one will not return, a meeting will not take place, or there will be a rejection of an application or job.

Practice Techniques for Mastering Interpretation of States of Being Cards

When States of Being cards emerge in a reading, they invite deeper exploration that transcends literal interpretation. As a reader, you can move beyond surface meanings to uncover the complex energetic patterns that shape the inquirer's persistent conditions and reveal pathways for more conscious and intentional living.

To help you develop your intuition for interpretation of the cards, the following sections present question lists for common states of being questions.

State Quality Exploration

- What is the fundamental quality of this persistent state?
- How deeply is this condition influencing the inquirer?
- Is this state transitory or more enduring?
- What qualities characterize this mode of being?

- How does this state affect perception and awareness?
- How conscious is the person of this state of being?

State Function Inquiry

- What purpose might this state be serving?
- How is this condition affecting the inquirer's functioning?
- What need is being addressed through this state?
- What benefits or challenges does this state provide?
- How does this mode of being influence decision-making?
- What information or wisdom does this state offer?
- How might this condition be intentionally utilized?

State Balance Analysis

- Is this condition in healthy proportion or excessive?
- How is this state affecting decision-making and perception?
- What complementary state might bring greater balance?
- How might moderation be achieved if needed?
- What happens when this state becomes extreme?
- How might integration with other states create wholeness?

Transformational Potential Questions

- How might this state serve as a catalyst for growth?
- What wisdom or lesson is embedded in this condition?
- What potential for positive change exists within this state?
- How might conscious awareness transform this habitual mode?
- What gifts lie hidden within this persistent condition?

Agency and Choice Considerations

- How much control does the inquirer have over this state?
- What choices are available within this condition?
- What might shift or alter this persistent state?
- What patterns or triggers establish or maintain this state?
- What practices might modify this condition if desired?
- How might intentionality transform this habitual state?

CHAPTER 3

Interpreting Card Combinations

Foundational Principles

The true power of the Gypsy Oracle Cards lies in the centuries-old tradition of reading cards in combination. While individual card meanings provide a foundation, it is through their interactions, juxtapositions, and relationships that the cards reveal their profound wisdom and offer multidimensional insights into the inquirer's situation.

This combinatorial approach has always been central to the Gypsy Oracle tradition. Expert readers understand that cards modify, enhance, and transform each other when they appear together in a reading. The specific arrangements, commonly called "spreads", create contexts through which these interactions can be explored and interpreted. Some practitioners remain devoted to a single layout, finding that it provides consistent clarity, while others select spreads based on the specific nature of the question or the energetic quality of the moment.

Regardless of which layout you choose, seven fundamental principles consistently guide the interpretation of card combinations. I've organized these principles into a systematic framework that will transform how you understand card relationships:

1. Amplification – Enhancing and Intensifying Energies

    Positive cards amplify the constructive potential of other cards, while negative cards intensify challenges and shadow aspects.

2. Transformation – Catalysts of Change

    Cards in combination that indicate a significant change is possible or occurring.

3. Contradiction – Understanding Opposing Energies

    Cards with opposing energies that suggest underlying tension or challenges to be resolved.

4. Progression – Developmental Sequences

    The combination suggests a developmental sequence or a story unfolding through multiple stages or a process with clear phases.

5. Balance – Harmonizing Complementary Energics

    Combinations that point to the need for balance or integration between complimentary energies to achieve wholeness.

6. Proximity and influence Understanding Spatial Relationships

    The relative position of cards gives insight into the relationship to or influence on the whole.

7. Directional energy – Understanding Flow and Causality Orientation and flow between cards can suggest direction or causality.

The following sections explain each principle in depth, with practical examples suggesting how to interpret different combinations. At the end of each section, you'll find suggested practice methods designed to help you master and incorporate these principles into your readings. By working systematically through these concepts and internalizing these foundational principles, you'll develop an intuitive understanding of how cards interact, allowing for interpretations of remarkable depth and accuracy.

3.1 Amplification

Enhancing and Intensifying Energies

Amplification occurs when card combinations create a more powerful, enhanced effect. It occurs when cards with complementary or similar energies strengthen each other's potential and expand their significance to additional dimensions.

Through amplification:

- Positive cards enhance each other's constructive potential
- Negative cards intensify each other's challenging aspects
- Mixed combinations reveal both enhanced opportunities and exacerbated challenges

- Subtle energies become more pronounced and visible
- Hidden potentials emerge with greater clarity

Understanding Amplification Dynamics

Amplification operates through several distinct mechanisms:

1. Resonance: Cards with compatible energies naturally reinforce each other
2. Intensification: Similar cards strengthen the power of shared messages
3. Enhancement: Complementary cards bring out the best in each other
4. Exacerbation: Challenging cards magnify difficulties when combined
5. Elevation: Certain combinations transcend individual meanings to create something greater

When interpreting amplified combinations, consider how the combined energy differs from each card individually. Pay attention to:

- The quality of the amplified energy (more intense, more stable, more transformative)
- Whether the amplification creates constructive or challenging effects
- How the blended energy manifests across different life domains
- The sustainability of the intensified energy

- Whether the amplification reveals hidden potentials or hidden problems

Amplification Examples

Table 10 in the Quick Reference Guides section includes a comprehensive list of amplification scenarios. This section provides expanded explanations of selected scenarios to demonstrate how amplification principles work in practice.

Positive Amplifications

When positive cards combine, they enhance each other's constructive potential, creating exceptionally favourable conditions or beneficial energies that exceed what either card could generate alone.

Love & Relationship Amplifications: These combinations enhance romantic connections, deep emotional bonds, and harmonious partnerships. For example,

- **Fortune + Love:** This amplified combination creates exceptionally blessed romantic connections, where luck and affection enhance each other, potentially indicating a "soulmate" connection or extraordinarily harmonious relationship. The relationship brings deep emotional fulfilment and seems divinely favoured.

- **Friend + Faithfulness:** This combination amplifies trustworthy support and unwavering loyalty, suggesting relationships characterized by exceptional

Interpreting Card Combinations

reliability and sincere dedication. These connections provide a foundation of security that remains steadfast through life's challenges.

Personal Development Amplifications: These combinations enhance personal growth, healing potential, and inner resources for positive transformation. For example,

- **Doctor + Scholar:** This pairing amplifies the healing potential of knowledge, suggesting that intellectual understanding combined with healing expertise creates profound transformation. It indicates exceptional skill in identifying root causes and applying effective remedies.

- **Hope + Joyfulness:** This amplification creates extraordinary optimism and heartfelt happiness, suggesting a particularly resilient positive outlook that can transform circumstances through the power of perspective. This combination indicates an ability to find light in even the darkest situations.

Prosperity & Success Amplifications: These combinations enhance material abundance, fortunate circumstances, and conditions for achievement. For example,

- **Fortune + Money:** This powerful amplification indicates exceptional financial luck and abundant prosperity, suggesting wealth that comes both through effort and fortunate circumstances. This combination can indicate windfall profits or unexpected financial opportunities.

- **Lord + House:** This amplification indicates powerful protection and exceptional stability, suggesting leadership that creates security and prosperity for all involved. This combination often appears when solid foundations combine with wise governance to create lasting success.

Negative Amplifications

When challenging cards combine, they intensify each other's difficult energies, revealing deeper layers of complexity in problematic situations.

Conflict & Opposition Amplifications: These combinations enhance adversarial energies, betrayals, and challenging interactions. For example,

- **Enemy + Foe:** This amplification creates a situation of intensified opposition and hostile intent, suggesting attacks from multiple directions or particularly determined adversaries. This combination indicates a need for exceptional vigilance and strategic defence.

- **Falseness + Despair:** Together these cards amplify deception leading to intense emotional distress, suggesting betrayals that create particularly painful jealousy or desperation. This combination indicates situations where trust has been profoundly violated.

Loss & Ending Amplifications: These combinations enhance experiences of conclusion, grief, and the processes of letting go. For example,

Interpreting Card Combinations

- **Death + Widower:** These cards together amplify definitive endings and profound mourning, suggesting particularly final separations followed by intense grieving. This combination indicates completions that require extensive emotional processing before moving forward.

- **Sorrow + Sighs:** This combination amplifies grief and unfulfilled longing, suggesting particularly painful emotional states characterized by both acute loss and persistent yearning. This amplification indicates deep emotional wounds that create ongoing distress.

Difficulty & Challenge Amplifications: These combinations enhance obstacles, limitations, and complex challenges requiring significant effort to overcome. For example,

- **Malady + Melancholy:** These cards enhance each other to indicate particularly debilitating conditions accompanied by emotional heaviness, suggesting situations where physical and emotional difficulties compound each other. This indicates healing journeys requiring attention to both body and spirit.

- **Prison + Haughtiness:** This amplification creates restriction made more difficult by pride, suggesting confinement that is particularly challenging because of resistance to accepting limitations. This indicates situations where excessive self-importance makes necessary constraints feel even more confining.

Mixed Amplifications

Some of the most interesting amplifications occur when cards of different qualities combine, revealing both enhanced opportunities and exacerbated challenges.

Growth Through Challenge Amplifications: These combinations enhance transformative potential emerging through difficult circumstances. For example,

- **Misfortune + Hope:** This combination amplifies optimism in the face of disaster, suggesting exceptional resilience and the ability to maintain faith despite devastating circumstances. This indicates situations where maintaining positive expectation becomes a powerful tool for overcoming setbacks.

- **Death + Child:** This amplification creates particularly powerful transformation and rebirth, suggesting endings that directly enable remarkably fresh beginnings. This indicates situations where complete release creates the conditions for entirely new potential to emerge.

Balanced Tension Amplifications: These combinations enhance the creative potential that emerges when complementary opposites are held in dynamic equilibrium. For example,

- **Journey + House:** This combination enhances the dynamic between movement and stability, suggesting particularly meaningful exploration that ultimately strengthens foundations. This indicates situations where travel or transitions serve to reinforce rather than undermine security.

- **Lord + Servant:** Together these cards enhance the balance between authority and service, suggesting particularly effective leadership that includes both command and support. This indicates situations where the ability to both direct and assist creates exceptional results.

Tips for Incorporating Amplifications in Readings

When discussing amplifications with inquirers, several approaches can be particularly helpful:

1. **Intensity awareness**: Help the inquirer understand the heightened energy present in their situation, whether challenging or beneficial
2. **Synergistic potential**: Highlight how combining certain energies or approaches in their life creates something greater than either alone
3. **Enhanced opportunity**: Emphasize particularly powerful positive combinations that represent exceptional potential or good fortune
4. **Exacerbated challenge**: Gently inform about how certain difficult aspects of their situation may be intensifying each other

5. **Balance strategies**: Offer guidance on how to work with intensified energies in balanced, sustainable ways

By recognizing and interpreting amplifications skillfully, readers can help inquirers understand both the exceptional opportunities and particular challenges present in their situation, offering insights into how energies combine to create powerful effects that transcend individual influences.

Conclusion: Amplification as a Window to Deeper Understanding

Amplification represents one of the most fundamental principles in Sibilla card interpretation, revealing how energies interact, enhance, and intensify each other to create more powerful effects than any card alone could indicate. By understanding these dynamics, readers can offer deeper insights into both the exceptional opportunities and particular challenges present in any situation.

This recognition of amplified energies exemplifies another distinctive strength of the Sibilla tradition and honours the truth that life's energies rarely operate in isolation, they combine, enhance, diminish, or transform each other in complex ways that create our lived experience. By becoming attuned to these amplification patterns, readers can help inquirers recognize both extraordinary potential and heightened challenges, offering guidance that acknowledges the full complexity and richness of human experience.

The skilled Sibilla reader, therefore, functions not just as an interpreter of individual symbols but as a guide to understanding intricate energetic relationships. This ability to perceive and explain how forces amplify each other enables readers to provide inquirers with more profound insight into the intensified energies shaping their journey, empowering them to navigate both exceptional opportunities and particular challenges with greater awareness and intentionality.

Practice Techniques for Mastering Interpretation of Amplifications

To effectively work with amplifications in your readings, consider these approaches:

Identify Resonant Energies

Look for cards that naturally enhance each other through:

- Similar qualities that intensify when combined
- Complementary energies that bring out the best in each other
- Contrasting forces that create powerful balance or tension
- Thematic connections that deepen meaning when joined

Assess Amplification Quality

Determine whether the amplification creates:

- Constructive enhancement that improves situations
- Challenging intensification that exacerbates difficulties

- Balanced tension that creates growth through opposition
- Transformative synergy that creates something greater than the sum of its parts

Gauge Amplification Strength

Consider the degree of amplification present:

- Mild enhancement that subtly strengthens existing energies
- Moderate amplification that significantly boosts potential
- Powerful intensification that dramatically transforms the reading
- Extraordinary synergy that creates entirely new meaning

Explore Domain-Specific Effects

Examine how the amplified energy manifests across different life areas:

- How does this combination affect relationships differently than work?
- Does this amplification have greater impact on emotional versus practical matters?
- Are there specific contexts where this enhanced energy is particularly powerful?
- How might this intensified energy manifest differently for different personality types?

Consider Sustainability

Assess whether the amplified energy is sustainable or temporary:

- Can this intensified energy be maintained long-term?
- What might cause this enhanced state to diminish or change?
- How can the inquirer work with this amplified energy responsibly?
- What balance might be needed to make this intensification sustainable?

3.2 Transformation

Catalysts of Change

Transformation in card combinations goes deeper than progression or amplification. It reveals the specific mechanisms by which change occurs—the catalyst, the process, and the emergence of something fundamentally new. When cards with transformative relationships appear together, they show not just what changes, but how and why the transformation unfolds.

Through transformation combinations:

- Challenging states become converted into constructive potentials
- Limiting circumstances catalyze unexpected growth
- Conflicting energies resolve into higher synthesis
- Apparent obstacles become pathways to liberation
- Loss creates space for renewal and rebirth

Understanding Transformation Dynamics

Transformation operates through several distinct mechanisms:

1. **Catalytic change**: One energy directly triggers transformation in another
2. **Alchemical conversion**: Difficult experiences transmute into wisdom or growth

3. **Liberating release**: Limitations or endings create freedom for new developments
4. **Threshold crossing**: Movement from one state to a fundamentally different condition
5. **Paradoxical reversal**: Apparent obstacles become the very means of breakthrough

When interpreting transformative combinations, consider not just the before and after states, but the precise mechanism of change. Pay attention to:

- The quality of transformation (healing, liberating, renewing, purifying)
- The catalyst that triggers or enables the transformation
- Whether the transformation occurs through addition or subtraction
- The depth and permanence of the change
- What must be surrendered for the transformation to occur

Transformational Combinations Examples

Table 11 in the Quick Reference Guides section includes a comprehensive list of transformation combinations. This section provides expanded explanations of selected transformations with examples of card pairings representing the change energy in a reading.

Death & Rebirth Transformations

These combinations reveal the profound process of complete ending followed by renewal, showing how dissolution creates the necessary space for new life to emerge. For example,

- **Death + Child:** The complete ending (Death) directly enables an entirely fresh beginning (Child), suggesting the total transformation of a situation that makes way for something entirely new and unburdened by the past. This powerful combination reveals the phoenix-like rebirth that can only emerge after complete surrender and release.

- **Sorrow + Joyfulness:** This combination illuminates how acute grief can transform into heartfelt happiness, revealing the alchemical process through which emotional pain transmutes into a more profound capacity for joy. The depth of sorrow becomes the very catalyst that creates expanded capacity for authentic happiness.

Liberation & Freedom Transformations

These combinations show how restriction or opposition can paradoxically become the very catalyst for liberation and new freedoms. For example,

- **Prison + Journey:** Restrictions or limitations are transformed through movement and progress, suggesting liberation from constraints or finding freedom despite apparent confinement. This combination reveals how boundaries that seem to restrict can become the very catalyst for exploration and expansion.

- **Enemy + Friend:** This transformative pairing shows how opposition can convert into alliance, revealing the alchemical process through which adversaries become supporters. The very tension and challenge created by an opponent becomes the catalyst for developing qualities that eventually create connection and mutual respect.

Healing & Restoration Transformations

These combinations illustrate how wounding or loss can initiate powerful healing processes that lead to greater wholeness than before. For example,

- **Thief + Doctor:** What has been taken or lost becomes the catalyst for healing, where the experience of betrayal or loss provides crucial insights for restoration and recovery. This combination reveals how the wound itself contains the medicine, with the very experience of loss creating the conditions for deeper wholeness.

- **Despair + Hope:** The journey from emotional darkness to optimism, where the deepest negative emotions are transformed through inner vision and faith in possibilities, creating profound personal development. This combination reveals how the very depths of jealousy and negativity can become the catalyst for extraordinary resilience.

Wisdom & Insight Transformations

These combinations reveal how experience, even difficult experience, can be transmuted into deeper understanding and wisdom. For example,

- **Falseness + Scholar:** This pairing reveals the transformation from deception to wisdom, showing how encountering insincerity can catalyze dedicated pursuit of truth. The disorientation of being misled becomes the very impetus for committed learning and discernment.

- **Young Woman + Old Woman:** This combination illuminates the transformation from potential to wisdom, revealing the alchemical process through which developing qualities mature into experienced insight. The journey itself becomes the catalyst for transforming possibility into embodied knowledge.

Relationship Transformations

These combinations show how connections between people can fundamentally change in nature through catalytic experiences. For example,

- **Foe + Friend:** This transformation shows how competitiveness can evolve into collaboration, revealing the process through which rivalry becomes the very catalyst for developing mutual respect. The tension between competitors creates the challenges that eventually forge authentic connection.

- **Prison + Reunion:** This transformation shows how confinement can eventually lead to reconciliation, revealing the way that limitation and separation often precede meaningful reconnection. The experience of isolation becomes the very catalyst that creates appreciation for togetherness.

Personal Growth Transformations

These combinations reveal the catalytic processes that fundamentally change one's internal landscape and way of being in the world. For example,

- **Prison + Child:** This transformation shows how restriction can eventually birth new potential, revealing the way that confinement often creates the pressure necessary for complete reinvention. The limitations themselves become the very catalyst for innocent new beginning.

- **Melancholy + Joyfulness:** This transformation shows how reflective sadness can transform into heartfelt happiness, revealing the necessary role of introspective grief in developing capacity for authentic joy. The depth created through melancholy becomes the very vessel that can hold true happiness.

Career and Financial Transformations

These combinations illustrate how professional and financial circumstances can undergo fundamental shifts through catalytic experiences. For example,

- **Misfortune + Money:** This combination illustrates how disaster can transform into prosperity, showing the counterintuitive way that financial catastrophe often precedes more conscious wealth development. The complete reset created by misfortune becomes the very foundation for healthier financial patterns.

- **Waiting + Fortune:** This pairing reveals how patient anticipation transforms into exceptional luck, showing the alchemical way that suspended action creates receptivity to fortunate timing. The discipline of patience itself becomes the very quality that attracts favourable circumstances.

Tips for Using Transformations in Readings

There are several approaches you can use to assist in discussing transformative combinations with inquirers.

1. **Identify catalysts**: Help inquirers recognize the specific triggers or catalysts currently active in their situation
2. **Embrace change**: Emphasize the transformative journey rather than just the beginning and end states, highlighting the value of the process itself

3. **Surrender guidance**: Gently explore what might need to be released or surrendered for the transformation to proceed
4. **Embrace contradictions**: Help inquirers appreciate the counterintuitive aspects of their situation, where challenges may actually be creating opportunities
5. **Give hope**: Offer the perspective that difficult experiences often contain precisely the elements needed for growth and transmutation

By recognizing and interpreting transformations skillfully, readers can help inquirers understand the processes at work in their lives, offering insights into how challenging experiences often contain precisely the elements needed for profound personal evolution and circumstantial change.

Conclusion – Transformation as a Path to Positive Outcomes

This focus on transformation embodies one of the most distinctive strengths of the Sibilla tradition, its emphasis on guiding the inquirer toward positive outcomes, even in the face of challenges. Unlike systems that merely predict events, Sibilla reading illuminates the transformative potential in every situation, empowering inquirers to consciously participate in their own evolution. The cards reveal not just what is happening, but how current circumstances can be transformed into more favourable conditions through awareness and intentional engagement.

This approach honours the truth that life's most significant developments often emerge through surprising catalysts, apparent obstacles that become pathways, losses that create space for greater gain, endings that enable fresh beginnings. By becoming attuned to these transformative patterns, readers can help inquirers recognize the hidden potential within their most challenging experiences, offering guidance that illuminates the mysterious alchemy through which life's difficulties often become the very means of profound evolution and unexpected grace.

The art of Sibilla reading, therefore, is not fortune-telling but transformation-revealing, showing inquirers how they might navigate their circumstances with wisdom that turns challenge into opportunity and limitation into expansion. This empowering orientation makes transformation interpretation a vital skill for readers seeking to provide not just insight, but genuine guidance toward positive life development.

Practice Techniques for Mastering Recognition and Interpretation of Transformations

To effectively work with transformative combinations in your readings, consider these approaches:

Identify the Catalyst

Look carefully at what triggers or enables the transformation:

- Which card represents the catalytic force?
- Is the catalyst challenging or supportive in nature?
- What specific quality or energy enables the transformation?
- Is the catalyst external (circumstance) or internal (attitude)?

Understand the Process

Examine how the transformation unfolds:

- Does it occur through addition or subtraction?
- Is it a sudden shift or gradual evolution?

- What must be surrendered for the transformation to occur?
- What facilitates or impedes the transformative process?

Recognize the Metamorphosis

Identify the fundamental change taking place:

- How is the essential quality or energy being transmuted?
- What new potential is emerging from the transformation?
- Is something being revealed that was present all along?
- How permanent or temporary is the transformation?

Explore Paradoxical Elements

Consider the counterintuitive aspects of the transformation:

- How might apparent obstacles actually facilitate progress?
- In what ways might challenging experiences enable growth?
- How might limitation create unexpected freedom?
- Where might loss actually create space for greater gain?

Identify Required Conditions

Determine what circumstances support the transformation:

- What attitudes facilitate this transformative process?
- What external support might be necessary?
- What timing factors influence the transformation?
- What level of awareness helps or hinders the process?

3.3 Contradiction

Understanding Opposing Energies

The Gypsy Oracle Deck contains many archetypal cards that represent opposing energies or contradictory states. Understanding these contradictions can provide deeper insight into the dynamics at play in any situation, revealing the subtle tensions and forces that shape our experiences.

Far from indicating confusion or inconsistency, these contradictions reveal the complex interplay of opposing forces that exist within any significant life situation. When contradictory cards appear together, they illuminate the subtle tensions, polarities, and paradoxes that shape human experience.

Contradiction in card reading functions as a mirror reflecting the inherent complexity of life itself, where seemingly opposite forces often coexist and interact in ways that defy simple categorization. Like the complementary principles of yin and yang, contradictory cards reveal how opposing energies exist not in isolation but in dynamic relationship—each containing elements of the other and together forming a more complete picture of reality.

Understanding Contradictory Dynamics

Contradiction in card readings operates through several distinct mechanisms:

1. **Internal Tension**: Opposing desires, attitudes, or needs creating psychological conflict The inquirer may be experiencing conflicting desires or attitudes
2. **Transitional States**: Movement occurring between one condition or state and its opposite
3. **Balance Requirements**: Need for equilibrium between contrasting forces or approaches The reading may be suggesting finding middle ground between extremes
4. **Choice Points**: Situations requiring decision between contradictory paths The inquirer may need to choose between contradictory approaches
5. **Complex Realities**: Circumstances containing paradoxical or coexisting opposite elements The situation contains nuanced elements that aren't easily categorized

When interpreting contradictions, consider:

- The specific nature of the opposition between the cards
- Which aspect of contradiction (tension, transition, balance, choice, or complexity) seems most relevant
- How the contradiction manifests in the inquirer's specific situation
- Whether resolution or integration of the opposing energies is possible or desirable
- What wisdom might emerge from embracing rather than eliminating the contradiction

Major Contradictory Pairings

Table 12 in the Quick Reference Guides section includes a comprehensive list of contradictory pairings. This section provides expanded explanations of selected pairings to demonstrate how contradiction principles work in practice.

Commitment vs. Freedom Tensions

These combinations reveal the fundamental tension between connection and autonomy, showing how we simultaneously desire both stable bonds and personal freedom. For example,

- **Wedding + Prison:** This powerful contradictory pairing reveals the tension between formal commitment and personal freedom. The Wedding card represents joyful union and partnership, while Prison embodies restriction and loss of autonomy. Together, they illuminate how commitment can simultaneously represent both loving connection and perceived constraint.

- **Journey + House:** This contradictory pairing illuminates the tension between exploration and stability, movement and rootedness. The Journey card represents transition and movement toward new horizons, while House embodies security and established foundation. Together, they reveal the opposing pulls of adventure and stability that many experience throughout life.

Trust vs. Deception Tensions

These combinations expose the delicate balance between openness and protection, revealing how vulnerability creates both the possibility for deep connection and the risk of betrayal. For example,

- **Faithfulness + Thief:** This contradictory pairing exposes the tension between loyalty and betrayal. The Faithfulness card represents unwavering reliability and trustworthy support, while Thief embodies betrayal of trust and hidden agendas. Together, they illuminate how vulnerability through trust creates the very possibility of betrayal.

- **Friend + Foe:** This contradictory pairing reveals the thin line between alliance and enmity. The Friend card represents loyal companionship and genuine care, while Foe embodies opposition and conflict. Together, they illuminate the complex and sometimes shifting nature of human relationships.

Emotional Polarity Tensions

These combinations illuminate the full spectrum of human emotional experience, showing how seemingly opposite feelings often exist in close proximity or even give meaning to each other. For example,

- **Joyfulness + Sorrow:** This contradictory pairing illuminates the full spectrum of human emotional experience. The Joyfulness card represents heartfelt happiness and celebration, while Sorrow embodies grief and emotional pain. Together, they reveal the bittersweet nature of life's most meaningful experiences.

- **Hope + Despair:** This contradictory pairing reveals the tension between optimistic expectation and overwhelming negativity. The Hope card represents positive vision and faith in possibilities, while Despair embodies emotional darkness and perceived impossibility. Together, they illuminate the psychological tug-of-war between optimism and pessimism.

Service vs. Self Tensions

These combinations highlight the complex dynamics between caring for others and honouring one's own needs, showing how self-care and other-care must be balanced. For example,

- **Servant + Haughtiness:** This contradictory pairing highlights the tension between humble service and proud self-importance. The Servant card represents supportive assistance and attending to others' needs, while Haughtiness embodies pride and elevated sense of status. Together, they reveal complex attitudes about helping relationships.

- **Gift + Money:** This contradictory pairing illuminates the tension between freely giving and calculated exchange. The Gift card represents generosity without obligation, while Money embodies calculated value and careful accounting. Together, they reveal differing approaches to resources that often create tension within relationships.

Security vs. Vulnerability Tensions

These combinations reveal the delicate balance between protection and openness, showing how both safety and risk-taking are necessary for a fully lived life. For example,

- **Soldier + Child:** This contradictory pairing highlights the tension between protective strength and innocent vulnerability. The Soldier card represents protection and vigilant defence, while Child embodies innocence and unguarded openness. Together, they reveal the delicate balance between security measures and maintaining openness to new experiences.

- **Fortune + Malady:** This contradictory pairing reveals the paradoxical relationship between good luck and vulnerability. The Fortune card represents unexpected opportunities and favourable circumstances, while Malady embodies weakness and periods of vulnerability. Together, they illuminate how good fortune and difficulty often coexist or follow each other in life's cycles.

Tips for Interpretation of Contradiction in Reading

Contradiction Analysis Process

1. **Identify Primary Tensions** Begin by noting which cards create strong contradictions or oppositions:

- Which cards represent clearly opposing energies or states?
- How does each contradiction relate to the inquirer's situation?
- Which type of contradiction (internal tension, transition, balance need, choice point, or complexity) seems most relevant?

2. **Explore Manifestations** Consider how the contradiction might be manifesting in the inquirer's experience:
   - How might the inquirer be experiencing this contradiction internally?
   - Where might this contradiction be creating external tension in relationships or situations?
   - Is the contradiction currently conscious or operating beneath awareness?
   - Is one side of the contradiction being acknowledged while the other is being denied?

3. **Assess Resolution Possibilities** Consider whether and how the contradiction might be resolved:
   - Does this contradiction require choosing one side over the other?
   - Might integration or balance between the opposites be possible?
   - Is this a transitional contradiction that will naturally resolve over time?
   - Is this a fundamental paradox that requires acceptance rather than resolution?

4. **Identify Wisdom Potential** Look for the deeper insight or wisdom that might emerge through the contradiction:
   - What understanding becomes possible only by acknowledging both sides?
   - What growth opportunity does navigating this contradiction present?
   - How might consciously engaging with this tension lead to greater wholeness?
   - What new perspective might emerge from holding apparent opposites simultaneously?

Spread-Specific Contradiction Considerations

Different types of spreads reveal contradictions in ways that require specific interpretative approaches.

Cross Spread Contradictions

In the traditional cross spread, contradictions can appear in several significant relationships:

Center-Position Contradictions

When the central card contradicts cards in other positions, this reveals tension between core themes and surrounding factors
   - Center-Past contradictions suggest moving away from or transforming previous conditions

- Center-Future contradictions indicate emerging tensions or coming transitions
- Center-Obstacle contradictions show how what blocks progress may actually contain elements of the goal
- Center-Advice contradictions reveal how guidance may require embracing apparent opposites

Diagonal Contradictions

Contradictions between cards on diagonal axes (Past-Obstacle or Advice-Future) reveal subtler tensions

- Past-Obstacle diagonal contradictions show how history creates current challenges through pendulum swings
- Advice-Future diagonal contradictions suggest how guidance may create unexpected complexities when implemented

Cardinal Opposition Contradictions

Direct contradictions between Past-Future or Obstacle-Advice reveal fundamental polarities

- Past-Future contradictions highlight transitions between opposing states over time
- Obstacle-Advice contradictions show how the solution often involves embracing what seems most opposite to the problem

Linear Spread Contradictions

In linear spreads (3-card, 5-card, etc.), contradictions between adjacent cards take on special significance:

Adjacent Contradictions

Contradictions between neighbouring cards suggest direct transitions between opposing states .These adjacencies often indicate that one state is transforming into its opposite. The card order reveals the direction of transformation (which state is giving way to which).

Bookend Contradictions

Contradictions between the first and last cards in the spread reveal the overall journey or transformation. These oppositions show the complete arc from beginning to end and often represent completion of a full cycle of experience.

Central Tensions

In odd-numbered spreads, contradictions involving the middle card reveal core tensions. The central card often mediates between opposing energies on either side and the middle card contradictions highlight the heart of the matter requiring integration.

Conclusion: Contradiction as a Window into Life's Complexity

Contradiction in Sibilla Oracle readings reveals the complex interplay of opposing forces that shape human experience.

By attending to the tensions, transitions, balances, choices, and complexities created by contradictory cards, readers can unveil layers of meaning that more accurately reflect life's inherent paradoxes and polarities.

This recognition of contradictory energies highlights another distinctive strength of the Sibilla tradition, its embrace of paradox and complexity rather than oversimplification. This nuanced approach recognizes that meaning often emerges precisely at the points where apparent opposites meet in the dynamic space between seemingly contradictory states. Like the richness that emerges when complementary flavours combine, the wisdom revealed through contradictory cards offers depth and subtlety unavailable through simpler, more linear interpretations.

The masterful Sibilla reader, therefore, serves not as a dispenser of simplistic answers but as a guide through life's inherent complexities. By developing sensitivity to contradictions, readers can offer insights that honour the full complexity of human experience rather than reducing it to oversimplified either/or frameworks. Through embracing rather than resolving contradiction, the cards become a mirror reflecting life as it truly is—a rich tapestry woven from threads that include both light and shadow, joy and sorrow, freedom and commitment, in patterns more complex and beautiful than any single thread could create alone.

Practice Techniques for Mastering Readings with Contradictions

Dialogical Approach

Facilitate an imaginary dialogue between the contradictory cards:

- "If Wedding could speak to Prison, what would it say? How would Prison respond?"
- Explore how the opposing energies might communicate with each other
- Look for potential common ground or integration points that emerge through dialogue

This technique brings the contradiction to life, revealing how opposing energies might find relationship rather than remaining in opposition.

Both/And Questioning

Help inquirers move beyond either/or thinking through deliberate both/and exploration:

- "How might both Joyfulness and Sorrow be valid and present in this situation?"
- "What would it look like to honour both Journey and House energies in your life?"
- "How might both Faithfulness and Thief energies be operating in this relationship?"

This approach expands perspective beyond binary thinking to more nuanced understanding.

Paradox Meditation

Invite contemplation of the paradoxical wisdom that emerges through contradiction:

- "What wisdom becomes visible only when we hold both Wedding and Prison together?"
- "What understanding emerges when we acknowledge both Friend and Foe simultaneously?"
- "What truth reveals itself in the space between Servant and Haughtiness?"

This contemplative technique accesses the deeper wisdom that often lives in apparent contradiction.

Integration Visioning

Help inquirers imagine how contradictory energies might be harmonized or integrated:

- "What would it look like to create commitment that enhances rather than restricts freedom?"

- "How might you develop trust that includes appropriate awareness of vulnerability?"
- "What would a balanced approach incorporating both protection and openness involve?"

This practical technique moves from understanding contradiction to envisioning potential resolution.

3.4 Progression

Developmental Sequences

Progression sequences reveal how energies evolve and transform over time, mapping journeys of growth, healing, transformation, or decline. By identifying these sequential patterns, readers can provide deeper insights into the natural unfolding of situations, relationships, and personal development. Recognizing when card combinations suggest a developmental sequence, a story unfolding through multiple stages or a process with clear phases, moves beyond static interpretations to reveal the dynamic narratives embedded within spreads.

When multiple cards appear in a logical developmental order, they often tell a cohesive story with a beginning, middle, and end. These sequences can illuminate:

- Natural evolution of situations or relationships
- Transformative processes that require passing through specific phases
- Healing journeys with recognizable emotional or psychological stages
- Developmental pathways for personal or professional growth
- Cycles of change that follow archetypal patterns

Understanding Progression Dynamics

Progression dynamics differ from simple card combinations in several important ways:

1. **Temporal logic**: Cards follow a sequence that makes sense chronologically
2. **Developmental coherence**: Each stage builds upon or emerges from the previous
3. **Narrative clarity**: Together, the cards tell a cohesive story with a beginning, middle, and end
4. **Transformative potential**: The sequence reveals how one state or condition evolves into another
5. **Archetypal patterns**: The progression often follows recognizable patterns of human experience

When interpreting progressions, consider both the significance of each individual stage and how they connect to form a meaningful whole. Pay attention to:

- How each stage prepares for or enables the next
- Whether the sequence represents constructive development or challenging decline
- If the progression feels complete or if stages appear to be missing
- How the inquirer's current situation fits within the larger sequence

Classic Progression Examples

Table 13 in the Quick Reference Guides section includes a comprehensive list of progression sequences. This section provides expanded explanations of selected sequences to demonstrate how progression principles work in practice.

Relationship Progressions

These sequences reveal the natural evolution of connections between people, showing how relationships develop, deepen, heal, or dissolve over time. For example,

- **Conversation + Reunion + Wedding:** This three-card progression tells the story of dialogue leading to reconciliation and eventually to formal commitment, mapping a relationship journey from communication to reconnection to lasting union. It shows how open exchange creates the foundation for healing past divisions, which then enables deeper commitment.

- **Love + Falseness + Sorrow + Death:** This progression maps the painful dissolution of a relationship, from initial affection through deception to heartbreak and finally complete ending. It shows how betrayal of trust can lead to a relationship's demise through predictable emotional stages.

Personal Development Progressions

These sequences chart the journey of individual growth and maturation, revealing how character and capability evolve through different life stages. For example,

- **Child + Young Woman + Old Woman:** This classic sequence represents the natural development of feminine wisdom through life stages, from innocence through developing potential to mature wisdom. It shows how experience gradually transforms potential into wisdom.

- **Frivolity + Thought + Constancy + Service:** This progression shows the maturing of character from carefree attitude through reflection to reliability and ultimately selfless contribution. It maps a journey of increasing depth and substance in one's approach to life.

Emotional Healing Progressions

These sequences illuminate the process of emotional recovery and renewal, showing how we move through difficult feelings toward greater wholeness. For example,

- **Despair + Melancholy + Consolation + Hope:** This progression charts an emotional healing journey from destructive jealousy through reflective sadness to finding comfort and eventually renewed optimism. It demonstrates how healing often requires moving through, rather than avoiding, difficult emotions.

- **Falseness + Prison + Thought + Consolation:** This progression reveals how confronting deception can lead to a period of restriction and introspection that ultimately results in clarity and comfort. It shows the transformative power of facing hard truths.

Interpreting Card Combinations

Transformational Progressions

These sequences reveal profound change processes that fundamentally alter circumstances or identity, showing how complete transformation unfolds through distinct stages. For example,

- **Thief + Prison + Death + Child:** This powerful sequence shows how loss leads to restriction, which forces a complete ending, ultimately making way for an entirely new beginning—a profound transformation narrative. It reveals the phoenix-like rebirth that can follow complete surrender.

- **Death + Room + Thought + Journey:** This sequence reveals how endings create space for contemplation, which eventually leads to new movement and exploration. It shows the importance of solitude and reflection in the transition between life chapters.

Tips for Using Progressions in Readings

When discussing progressions with inquirers, several approaches can be particularly helpful:

1. **Narrative framing**: Present the progression as a story unfolding, helping the inquirer see their situation within a larger narrative arc
2. **Developmental context**: Normalize challenges by showing how they're natural parts of larger growth processes

3. **Stage awareness**: Help the inquirer recognize which stage they're currently experiencing and what it's preparing them for
4. **Phase-specific guidance**: Offer advice tailored to the particular phase the inquirer is navigating
5. **Preview upcoming stages**: Gently prepare the inquirer for what may lie ahead, empowering them to navigate future phases more consciously

By recognizing and interpreting progressions skillfully, readers can offer inquirers profound insights into the developmental nature of their experiences, highlighting both the purpose of current challenges and the potential transformations that await as they continue their journey.

Conclusion: Progression as a Map of Life's Unfolding

Progression analysis represents one of the most sophisticated approaches to Sibilla card interpretation, revealing the dynamic, evolving nature of human experience. By identifying these developmental sequences in readings, practitioners can offer deeper wisdom about how situations naturally unfold and transform over time.

This temporal approach exemplifies another distinctive strength of the Sibilla tradition, its understanding of life as a journey with recognizable phases, rather than as a series of static moments. Sibilla readings reveal the narrative arcs and developmental pathways that connect past, present, and future. This approach honours the truth that life is not static—it flows through recognizable patterns and phases, each serving a purpose in our larger development. By becoming fluent in the language of progressions, readers can help inquirers understand not just where they are, but where they've been, where they're heading, and how each stage serves the larger journey of growth and transformation.

Practice Techniques for Mastering Progressions in Readings

To effectively work with progressions in your readings, consider these approaches:

Identify Natural Sequences

Look for cards that form logical narrative sequences according to:

- Temporal order (what naturally comes before or after)
- Developmental stages (natural evolution of processes)
- Cause and effect relationships (how one state leads to another)
- Archetypal patterns (classic human journeys)

Locate the Inquirer in the Sequence

Determine where the inquirer is currently positioned within the progression:

- Have they completed initial stages and are moving into middle phases?
- Are they stuck at a particular point in the sequence?
- Are they nearing completion of the full progression?
- Are they moving through the progression in a balanced way or rushing certain stages?

Identify Missing Stages

Sometimes progressions appear incomplete or show gaps:

- What stages might be missing from the sequence?
- Are these stages being avoided or unconsciously skipped?
- Would the progression flow more naturally if certain steps were included?
- Do missing stages explain why progress feels blocked or incomplete?

Examine Timing and Pacing

Consider how the progression is unfolding temporally:

- Are certain stages moving too quickly or too slowly?
- Is there a natural timing to this particular sequence?
- Are external factors accelerating or delaying the progression?
- Does the inquirer need to slow down or speed up certain phases?

Explore Potential Variations

Progressions aren't always linear; they may include:

- Cyclical patterns that repeat at higher levels
- Spiralling development that revisits themes with greater awareness
- Parallel sequences that unfold simultaneously
- Branching possibilities where different paths might emerge

3.5 Balance

Harmonizing Complementary Energies

Among the most nuanced interpretative principles in Gypsy Oracle Cards is the concept of balance, how certain card combinations reveal the need for equilibrium between complementary or opposing energies to create wholeness and harmony. These balanced combinations illuminate the dynamic tensions that exist within all aspects of life, suggesting that integration, rather than elimination of differences, often creates the most sustainable and fulfilling outcomes.

Balance in card combinations reveals more than mere coexistence of different energies; it points to the synergistic potential that emerges when seemingly contradictory forces are held in creative tension. When cards with balancing relationships appear together, they show how complementary qualities can enhance each other, creating a whole greater than the sum of its parts.

Through balance combinations:

- Opposing qualities find harmonious integration
- Complementary energies enhance each other
- Excessive tendencies receive natural correction
- One-sided approaches become more holistic
- Sustainable equilibrium emerges from apparent contradictions

Understanding Balance Dynamics

Balance operates through several distinct mechanisms:

1. **Complementary opposition**: Contrasting qualities that complete each other
2. **Dynamic tension**: Opposing forces creating productive equilibrium
3. **Compensatory pairing**: Qualities that provide what the other lacks
4. **Integrative synthesis**: Seemingly contradictory elements forming a unified whole
5. **Corrective balance**: One energy moderating the excess of another

When interpreting balance combinations, consider how the paired energies interact to create equilibrium. Pay attention to:

- The specific qualities being brought into balance
- Whether one energy is currently excessive or deficient
- How the balanced state differs from either extreme
- What new potential emerges through this integration
- How sustainable the equilibrium might be over time

Major Balance Combinations

Table 14 in the Quick Reference Guides section includes a comprehensive list of balance combinations. This section provides expanded explanations of selected combinations to demonstrate how balance principles work in practice.

Structure & Flexibility Balances

These combinations reveal the need for equilibrium between order and spontaneity, showing how both stability and adaptability are essential for sustainable growth. For example,

- **Constancy + Frivolity:** This pairing suggests finding equilibrium between reliability and playfulness, indicating the need to maintain serious commitments while also embracing light-heartedness. The steadfast dedication of Constancy prevents Frivolity from becoming irresponsible flightiness, while the light-hearted quality of Frivolity keeps Constancy from becoming rigid inflexibility.

- **House + Journey:** This pairing reveals the balance between stability and movement, suggesting the need to maintain secure foundations while embracing exploration and change. The grounded security of House prevents Journey from becoming aimless wandering, while the expansive exploration of Journey keeps House from becoming stagnant confinement.

Mind & Heart Balances

These combinations highlight the integration of intellectual understanding and emotional wisdom, showing how both thought and feeling contribute to complete knowing. For example,

- **Scholar + Lover:** This combination points to balancing intellectual pursuits with emotional and physical passion, suggesting that both mind and heart must be engaged for true fulfilment. The thoughtful analysis of Scholar prevents Lover from becoming blind infatuation, while the heartfelt devotion of Lover keeps Scholar from becoming cold intellectualism.

- **Old Woman + Child:** This pairing shows the balance between wisdom and innocence, indicating the importance of maintaining experienced perspective while embracing fresh wonder and openness. The mature insight of Old Woman prevents Child from becoming naive vulnerability, while the innocent curiosity of Child keeps Old Woman from becoming cynical rigidity.

Action & Receptivity Balances

These combinations reveal the dance between doing and being, showing how effective living requires both initiative and openness. For example,

- **Merchant + Gift:** This combination points to balancing strategic exchange with generous offering, suggesting the need to maintain practical acumen while embracing unearned abundance. The shrewd assessment of Merchant prevents Gift from becoming impractical generosity, while the unearned blessing of Gift keeps Merchant from becoming calculating manipulation.

- **Waiting + Journey:** This combination reveals the balance between patient anticipation and active movement, suggesting the wisdom of knowing when to remain still and when to advance. The calm expectancy of Waiting prevents Journey from becoming hasty rushing, while the forward momentum of Journey keeps Waiting from becoming passive stagnation.

Light & Shadow Balances

These combinations illuminate the integration of positive and challenging aspects of experience, showing how both optimism and realism contribute to wholeness. For example,

- **Hope + Melancholy:** This combination shows the balance between optimistic expectation and thoughtful sadness, suggesting the wisdom of maintaining faith while acknowledging emotional depth. The positive vision of Hope prevents Melancholy from becoming debilitating depression, while the reflective depth of Melancholy keeps Hope from becoming naive positivity.

- **Friend + Foe:** This combination points to balancing alliance with healthy vigilance, suggesting the need for open connection while maintaining appropriate discernment. The supportive trust of Friend prevents Foe from becoming paranoid suspicion, while the cautious assessment of Foe keeps Friend from becoming indiscriminate vulnerability.

Relationship Balances

These combinations reveal the complementary dynamics that create sustainable and fulfilling connections between people, showing how different qualities enhance each other in various types of relationships. For example,

- **Lover + Friend:** This balance shows the importance of passion complemented by companionship, suggesting that romantic relationships thrive when intense attraction exists alongside genuine friendship. The passionate devotion of Lover prevents Friend from becoming merely platonic connection, while the authentic camaraderie of Friend keeps Lover from becoming merely physical attraction.
- **Wedding + Journey:** This pairing reveals the balance between commitment and freedom, indicating that partnerships flourish when formal dedication coexists with continued growth and exploration. The binding quality of Wedding prevents Journey from becoming destabilizing wandering, while the expansive energy of Journey keeps Wedding from becoming constraining obligation.

Family & Social Balances

These combinations illuminate the complementary energies that create healthy family systems and social connections. For example,

- **Lord + Child:** This balance shows the importance of authority complemented by playfulness, suggesting that parental relationships thrive when clear leadership exists alongside joyful nurturing. The protective guidance of Lord prevents Child from becoming undisciplined vulnerability, while the innocent wonder of Child keeps Lord from becoming oppressive control.

- **Old Woman + Young Woman:** This combination points to balancing mature wisdom with developing potential, suggesting that intergenerational relationships thrive through mutual respect and exchange. The experienced insight of Old Woman prevents Young Woman from making unnecessary mistakes, while the fresh perspective of Young Woman keeps Old Woman from becoming rigid or outdated.

Inner Harmony Balances

These combinations reveal the complementary qualities needed for psychological wholeness and internal integration. For example,

- **Scholar + Frivolity:** This balance shows the importance of serious study complemented by playful lightness, suggesting that personal development thrives when depth of knowledge exists alongside joyful spontaneity. The intellectual rigour of Scholar prevents Frivolity from becoming shallow superficiality, while the carefree quality of Frivolity keeps Scholar from becoming dry intellectualism.
- **Hope + Sorrow:** This pairing reveals the balance between optimism and emotional honesty, indicating that authentic development requires both positive vision and willingness to feel difficult emotions.

The forward-looking quality of Hope prevents Sorrow from becoming debilitating grief, while the depth of Sorrow keeps Hope from becoming superficial positivity.

Professional & Financial Balances

These combinations highlight the complementary approaches needed for sustainable success and satisfaction in work and financial matters. For example,

- **Merchant + Doctor:** This balance shows the importance of strategic acumen complemented by healing expertise, suggesting that professional success comes through both effective exchange and genuine care. The transactional skill of Merchant prevents Doctor from becoming financially unsustainable service, while the healing focus of Doctor keeps Merchant from becoming exploitative commerce.
- **Money + Gift:** This balance shows the importance of abundant resources complemented by generous sharing, suggesting that financial wisdom includes both accumulation and circulation. The material prosperity of Money prevents Gift from becoming impractical generosity, while the freely given quality of Gift keeps Money from becoming miserly hoarding.

Tips for Interpreting Balance in Readings

When discussing balance combinations with inquirers, several approaches can be particularly helpful:

1. **Complementary awareness**: Help inquirers recognize how seemingly opposing qualities can actually enhance and complete each other
2. **Beyond either/or thinking**: Encourage movement beyond binary thinking toward both/and integration that honours the value in apparent opposites
3. **Sustainable wholeness**: Emphasize how balance creates more sustainable and fulfilling experiences than one-sided approaches
4. **Dynamic equilibrium**: Explain that balance is not static but a continual dance of complementary energies that responds to changing circumstances
5. **Higher synthesis**: Highlight how integration creates something greater than either quality alone could achieve, pointing to the emergent potential of balanced approaches

By recognizing and interpreting balances skillfully, readers can help inquirers understand the complementary dynamics at work in their lives, offering insights into how seemingly contradictory qualities often create the most sustainable and fulfilling approaches when held in creative tension.

Conclusion: Balance as the Path to Wholeness

Balance represents one of the most sophisticated principles in Sibilla card interpretation, revealing the harmonious integration possible when seemingly opposing energies are brought into creative relationship. By understanding these equilibrium dynamics, readers can offer deeper wisdom about how complementary qualities enhance rather than diminish each other, creating wholeness that transcends one-sided approaches.

This emphasis on balance exemplifies another distinctive strength of the Sibilla tradition, its recognition that well-being emerges not from extremes but from the skilful integration of complementary forces. The masterful Sibilla reader therefore becomes a guide to equilibrium, helping inquirers recognize where imbalances may exist and how opposing qualities might be brought into more harmonious relationship. By developing sensitivity to these balanced combinations, readers can offer guidance that moves beyond simplistic "either/or" thinking toward a more nuanced "both/and" wisdom, revealing the potential for integration that honors the value in seemingly contradictory qualities.

This approach recognizes that sustainable well-being rarely comes from extremes, it emerges from the dance between complementary forces, the creative tension between opposites held in dynamic balance. Through understanding these balance dynamics, the Sibilla tradition offers a profound path toward wholeness that embraces life's complexities rather than trying to eliminate them.

Practice Techniques for Recognizing and Interpreting Balances in Readings

To effectively work with balance combinations in your readings, consider these approaches:

Identify Complementary Tensions

Look for cards that create productive opposition through:

- Contrasting qualities that complete each other
- Apparent contradictions that actually enhance one another
- Qualities that provide what the other lacks
- Dynamic tensions that create sustainable equilibrium

Assess Current Imbalances

Determine whether equilibrium currently exists or if adjustment is needed:

- Is one quality overdeveloped and the other underdeveloped?

- Has the inquirer been emphasizing one aspect at the expense of another?
- Is there resistance to embracing one of the balancing energies?
- What might result from continued imbalance in this area?

Explore Integration Potential

Consider how the balanced energies might work together:

- What new possibility emerges when these qualities are integrated?
- How might each quality enhance rather than diminish the other?
- What higher synthesis becomes possible through this balance?
- How might integration create something greater than either quality alone?

Identify Balancing Practices

Suggest concrete ways to develop the underrepresented quality:

- What specific activities might cultivate the needed balance?
- How can the inquirer honour both energies in daily life?
- What small steps might begin the balancing process?

- Who might model this balanced approach for the inquirer?

Anticipate Integration Challenges

Consider potential difficulties in achieving balance:
- What resistance might emerge when embracing the complementary energy?
- What beliefs or fears might block integration?
- What external factors might hinder balanced expression?
- What support might facilitate the balancing process?

3.6 Proximity and Influence

Understanding Spatial Relationships

Among the most nuanced principles in Gypsy Oracle Card interpretation is the concept of proximity and influence—how the physical arrangement of cards within a spread creates meaningful relationships that can significantly affect their interpretation. This spatial dimension of card reading transcends individual card meanings, revealing the subtle energetic connections, tensions, and synergies that emerge through positional relationships.

Proximity in card spreads functions as a visual language that communicates how different energies interact, modify, and transform each other. The distance between cards, their alignment, opposition, or geometric patterns all contribute vital information about how these archetypal energies relate to one another in the inquirer's situation. Just as in human relationships, where physical proximity often indicates emotional closeness, the spatial arrangements of cards reveal the interconnected web of influences shaping the inquirer's circumstances.

Through proximity relationships:

- Adjacent energies blend and modify each other
- Opposing forces create tension or balance
- Geometric patterns reveal systemic dynamics
- Central themes emerge that organize surrounding influences

- Hierarchies of importance become visible through spatial arrangement

Understanding Proximity Dynamics

Proximity operates through several distinct mechanisms:

1. **Adjacent Influence**: Direct modification of card meanings through immediate proximity
2. **Positional Modification**: How location within a specific spread position affects interpretation
3. **Geometric Patterning**: Meaningful shapes formed by related cards
4. **Center-Periphery Relationships**: How core themes relate to surrounding influences
5. **Diagonal Connections**: Cross-connections that reveal hidden relationships

When interpreting proximity relationships, consider:

- The specific positions of cards relative to each other
- Whether cards occupy significant positions in the spread
- What patterns or shapes might be forming among related cards
- How distance affects the strength of influence between cards
- Whether cards are in harmonious or challenging relationships based on position

Major Proximity Principles

Adjacent Card Relationships

Direct Contact Influence

Cards that directly touch or share a common edge have the strongest mutual influence, often blending their meanings or significantly modifying each other. This immediate proximity suggests a direct relationship that cannot be ignored—these energies are actively engaging with each other in the inquirer's situation.

The influence of adjacent cards operates like two voices in close conversation—neither can speak without being heard and modified by the other. The proximity creates a third meaning that emerges from their interaction, something distinct from what either card would signify alone.

Examples:

Love + Falseness: When these cards are directly adjacent, the Love card's pure emotional connection becomes tainted by the deceptive quality of Falseness, suggesting romance clouded by dishonesty or illusion, rather than either quality existing independently.

Fortune + Prison: When touching, Fortune's abundant luck becomes confined or limited by Prison's restrictive energy, suggesting an opportunity that comes with significant constraints, rather than pure good fortune.

Doctor + Thief: In direct contact, Doctor's healing ability is compromised by Thief's taking energy, suggesting healthcare costs, stolen vitality, or treatments that cause side effects, creating a complex interaction rather than separate meanings.

Opposition Relationships

Polarized Energies

Cards that appear in opposite positions within a spread often represent contrasting forces or polarities that are seeking resolution or integration. This oppositional positioning suggests tension between these energies that creates a dynamic interplay in the inquirer's situation.

Opposition relationships operate like complementary colours that, while contrasting, actually enhance each other through their difference. The distance creates a magnetic field of tension that must be navigated or integrated for resolution to occur.

Examples:

House + Journey: When positioned on opposite sides of a spread, these cards reveal the fundamental tension between stability and movement, suggesting the inquirer is torn between secure foundations and the call to exploration.

Friend + Foe: In opposition, these cards highlight the thin line between alliance and enmity, suggesting relationships that could develop in either direction depending on how the inquirer navigates them.

Constancy + Surprise: Appearing in opposite positions, these cards reveal the struggle between reliable consistency and unexpected developments, challenging the inquirer to maintain stability while remaining open to the unforeseen.

Geometric Patterns

System Relationships

When three or more cards form recognizable geometric shapes (triangles, squares, lines), they create system relationships that reveal complex dynamics in the inquirer's situation. These patterns suggest interrelated factors that function as a unified system rather than isolated influences.

Geometric patterns operate like constellations in the night sky—their meaning emerges not just from the individual stars but from the shape they collectively form. These patterns create a structural understanding of how multiple factors interact in a systemic way.

Examples:

Triangular Patterns: When three cards form a triangle, they suggest a cyclical process or three interrelated aspects of a situation that continually influence each other. For example, a triangle formed by Lover + Foe + Wife suggests a classic romantic triangle with complex interrelationships.

Linear Arrangements: When three or more cards fall in a straight line (even across different rows), they suggest a clear progression or sequence of development. For example, a line formed by Child + Young Woman + Old Woman suggests a clear developmental progression.

Square Patterns: When four cards form a square or rectangle, they suggest a contained situation with clear boundaries and internal dynamics. For example, a square formed by House + Money + Gift + Fortune suggests material abundance and financial security on multiple levels.

Central Focus

Core Themes

The card at the center of a spread typically represents the core issue or central theme, with surrounding cards serving to modify, challenge, or support this central energy. This central positioning suggests the gravitational center around which all other influences orbit.

Central focus operates like the sun in a solar system—while the planets maintain their own identity, they are all defined by their relationship to the central star. The center card provides the essential context for understanding all other cards in the spread.

Examples:

Despair at Center: When Despair occupies the central position, all surrounding cards are coloured by its emotional intensity, suggesting a situation where jealousy or overwhelming emotions are the defining factor through which all other influences must be understood.

Wedding at Center: With Wedding in the central position, surrounding cards reveal different aspects of commitment and partnership, suggesting a situation where formal bonds are the primary lens through which all other factors should be interpreted.

Money at Center: When Money occupies the central position, surrounding cards reveal different aspects of material resources and value exchange, suggesting financial considerations are the gravitational center of the current situation.

Distance Gradients

Strength of Influence

The influence of cards diminishes with distance, creating a gradient of impact where cards farther apart have less direct effect on each other than those in close proximity. This distance gradient suggests varying levels of influence among the factors in a inquirer's situation.

Distance gradients operate like sound waves that grow fainter with distance—while the message may still be received, its impact and clarity diminish as distance increases. The varying strength of connections reveals which influences are most immediately impactful.

Examples:

First Degree Separation: Cards separated by just one position still maintain strong influence on each other, creating secondary relationships that modify the reading. For instance, in a line reading, the first and third cards have a significant relationship, though less immediate than adjacent cards.

Opposite Corners: In square spreads, cards in opposite corners have the least direct influence on each other, suggesting factors that are related but not in immediate interaction. These distant relationships often represent background tensions or potential future developments.

Cross-Spread Diagonals: In cross spreads, cards on the diagonal have an indirect but meaningful relationship, often revealing hidden connections between past influences and future obstacles, or between advice and the current situation.

Tips for Interpreting Proximity in Readings

Proximity Highlighting

After laying out the spread, physically highlight or mark adjacent cards to make their relationships more visible:

- Use small objects to mark particularly significant adjacencies
- Draw temporary lines connecting cards in geometric patterns
- Use position markers to emphasize standard positions in the spread

This visual enhancement helps both reader and inquirer recognize the web of relationships more clearly.

Relationship Dialogue

Create a dialogue between adjacent cards by personifying their energies:

- If these two adjacent cards could speak to each other, what would they say?
- How would they modify each other's message?
- What new wisdom emerges from their conversation?

This technique brings the proximity relationships to life, making their dynamic interaction more accessible.

Pattern Storytelling

When you identify geometric patterns, tell the story of how these interrelated factors create a system:

- How do the cards in a triangle influence each other in a cyclical way?
- What progression does a line of cards reveal?

- How do cards in a square contain and define a situation?

This narrative approach helps inquirers understand complex systemic dynamics through accessible stories.

Central Anchoring

Always return to the central card as an anchoring point throughout the reading:

- How does each card or pattern relate to the central theme?
- What aspects of the core issue do surrounding cards illuminate?
- How do surrounding influences modify the central concern?

This technique maintains coherence by continually relating all insights back to the central focus.

Reading Cross Spread Proximities

In the traditional cross spread, proximity creates a unique dynamic centered around the core card:

Cardinal Proximities (Above, Below, Left, Right)

The cards in direct contact with the central card in the four cardinal directions have the strongest modifying influence. Each represents a distinct dimension of influence: past (above), future (below), obstacles (right), and advice (left).

These four cards create a primary system around the central theme.

Diagonal Relationships

The diagonal relationship between past and obstacle reveals how historical factors create current challenges. The diagonal between future and advice shows how guidance shapes coming developments. These cross-connections reveal hidden influences not immediately apparent.

Expansion Patterns

When using multiple layers in a cross spread, cards in the same position across layers (e.g., all obstacle cards) create a developmental sequence

This layering shows the evolution of each influence over time or at different levels of manifestation

Conclusion: Deeper Understanding Through Spatial Dynamics

Proximity relationships in Gypsy Oracle readings reveal the intricate web of influences that shape the inquirer's circumstances. By attending to the spatial arrangement of cards, their adjacencies, oppositions, patterns, central focus, and distance gradients—readers can unveil layers of meaning that transcend individual card interpretations.

This dimensional approach recognizes that meaning emerges not just from what cards appear but from how they relate to each other in space. Like a constellation whose significance comes from the pattern of stars rather than each star in isolation, the proximity relationships in a spread reveal the interconnected system of influences at work in the inquirer's life.

By developing sensitivity to these spatial dynamics, readers can offer more nuanced, systemic, and holistic insights that honour the complex web of factors shaping human experience. Through this approach, the cards become not just individual messengers but a collective wisdom whose fullest expression emerges through their meaningful arrangement in relation to one another.

Practice Techniques for Mastering Proximity Relationships

Proximity Analysis Process

1. Identify Primary Adjacencies

   Begin by noting all cards that share a direct edge, as these represent the strongest immediate influences:
   - Which cards are directly touching?
   - How does each adjacent pair modify the meaning of both cards?
   - What new meaning emerges from their combined influence?

2. Map Geometric Patterns

   Look for meaningful shapes formed by three or more cards:
   - Are there triangles, lines, squares, or other patterns?
   - What system dynamics might these patterns represent?
   - How do cards within patterns relate to each other?

3. Analyze Positional Significance
   Consider how standard positions in the spread affect each card's meaning:
   - How does the core position influence the central card's significance?
   - Are cards in positions of past, future, obstacle, or advice?
   - How does positional meaning amplify or modify each card's inherent energy?
4. Examine Opposition Relationships
   Note cards in directly opposing positions:
   - What polarities or tensions do these oppositions create?
   - How might these opposing energies need to be integrated?
   - Do the oppositions suggest internal conflicts or external circumstances?
5. Assess Influence Gradients
   Consider how distance affects the strength of relationships:
   - Which relationships are strongest due to proximity?
   - Which are more distant background influences?
   - How do these varying levels of influence prioritize factors in the situation?

3.7 Directional Energy

Understanding Flow and Causality

In the sophisticated art of Gypsy Oracle Card interpretation, directional energy stands as one of the most subtle yet powerful principles—revealing how cards influence each other through vectors of causality, sequence, and energetic flow. Beyond static meanings and even beyond proximity relationships, directional energy illuminates the dynamic movement between archetypal forces, showing not just what influences are present but how they flow into and transform one another.

Directional energy in card reading functions as a language of process rather than state, revealing the paths through which circumstances evolve and transform. Like rivers flowing through a landscape, these directional currents show how one energy naturally leads to, creates, or transforms into another. By recognizing these vectors of influence, readers can discern not just what is happening in a inquirer's situation but how it is unfolding—the causal patterns and developmental sequences that shape their experience.

Through directional energy analysis:

- Cause-effect relationships become visible
- Sequential developments unfold in time
- Transformational pathways reveal themselves
- Energy flows illuminate natural progressions
- Causal chains show how circumstances evolve

Understanding Directional Dynamics

Directional energy operates through several distinct mechanisms:

Causal Sequences: One card directly causing or leading to another

Transformational Flows: One energy state morphing into another

Developmental Progressions: Natural evolution from one stage to the next

Cyclical Patterns: Recurring sequences that feed back into themselves

Conditional Relationships: "If-then" dynamics between cards

When interpreting directional energies, consider:

- The specific direction of influence between cards
- Whether the flow is natural or forced, harmonious or resistant
- How the sequence affects the ultimate outcome
- Whether the directional energy can be redirected or modified
- How both directions of flow reveal different aspects of the situation

Major Directional Energy Patterns

Causal Pathways

Direct Cause and Effect

When cards appear in sequence or in positions suggesting a causal relationship, they reveal how one circumstance directly leads to another. These pathways illuminate chains of events shaping the inquirer's situation, operating like dominoes—when one falls, it creates a force affecting what follows. Understanding these relationships reveals not just what's happening but why, and how circumstances inevitably connect.

Examples:

Journey → Fortune When Journey flows into Fortune, movement and change directly generate lucky circumstances. This directional flow suggests that taking action or stepping into new territory creates prosperity or opportunity. The causal relationship indicates that remaining stationary would prevent fortunate circumstances from manifesting.

Prison → Thief When Prison flows into Thief, restriction directly creates vulnerability to loss or exploitation. This directional flow suggests that limiting circumstances make one susceptible to having something taken away. The causal relationship indicates that constraint weakens boundaries or creates blind spots enabling theft or loss.

Transformational Sequences

Energy Transmutation

Some directional relationships reveal how one state naturally transforms into another, showing the evolution of energies through different expressions. These sequences illuminate how circumstances change their nature over time, operating like chemical reactions where elements combine to become something entirely new. Understanding these processes reveals the natural evolution of circumstances and how energies transmute from one form to another.

Examples:

Sorrow → Hope When Sorrow flows into Hope, acute grief naturally transforms into renewed optimism. This directional flow suggests a healing process where the full experience of loss eventually gives birth to fresh vision. The transformation indicates that properly processed grief contains within it the seeds of new possibilities.

Conversation → Wedding When Conversation flows into Wedding, dialog and exchange naturally transform into formal commitment. This directional flow suggests that meaningful communication creates the foundation for binding partnership. The transformation indicates that clear expression and listening naturally evolve toward structured agreement.

Developmental Progressions

Natural Evolution

Some directional relationships reveal the natural stages of development, showing how circumstances or people evolve through predictable phases. These progressions illuminate the organic unfolding of processes over time, operating like plant growth, following inherent patterns from seed to mature plant. Understanding these sequences reveals the natural life cycles of situations and relationships.

Examples:

Child → Young Woman → Old Woman This three-card directional flow reveals the natural developmental progression of feminine energy from innocent potential through developing capacity to mature wisdom. Each stage naturally flows into the next, showing the organic evolution of both people and projects through predictable phases of growth.

Service → Money → Gift This sequence reveals the progression from giving support to receiving value to generous sharing, showing the natural evolution of exchange energy. The directional flow demonstrates how service naturally creates value that then becomes available for generous sharing.

Cyclical Patterns

Recurring Sequences

Some directional relationships reveal cycles that continually repeat, showing patterns of energy that flow in circular rather than linear fashion. These cyclical patterns illuminate recurring dynamics that may continue until consciously interrupted, operating like seasons, continually moving through a sequence that eventually returns to its starting point. These cycles reveal repeated patterns that may be either constructive or limiting.

Examples:

Hope → Disappointment → Despair → New Hope This four-card cyclical flow reveals a common emotional pattern where optimistic expectations lead to disappointment when unmet, which deepens into despair before eventually giving birth to fresh hope. The cycle continues until the pattern is consciously recognized and transformed.

Friend → Foe → Friend This cyclical flow reveals the common pattern of relationships that oscillate between alliance and opposition. The cycle shows how trust naturally encounters challenges that, when navigated, can lead back to renewed connection.

Conditional Relationships

If-Then Dynamics

Some directional relationships reveal conditional circumstances where one card creates the conditions determining how another manifests. These if-then dynamics illuminate how certain factors shape the expression of others, operating like computer logic, where one factor determines how another will function. Understanding these dynamics reveals how certain cards create conditions influencing how other energies manifest.

Examples:

Money + Thief → Despair In this conditional relationship, the presence of Money determines how Thief affects the inquirer, with the combination leading to Despair. The directional flow suggests that financial resources, when stolen or lost, create intense emotional distress. The presence of Money as the conditional factor determines the particular manifestation of loss.

Prison + Friend → Consolation In this conditional flow, the presence of Prison determines how Friend affects the inquirer, with the combination leading to Consolation. The directional energy suggests that constraint or limitation, when accompanied by supportive connection, results in comfort despite difficulty. The presence of Prison as the conditional factor shapes how the friendship is experienced.

Spread-Specific Directional Considerations

Different spreads create unique directional flows that require specific interpretive approaches.

Linear Spread Directions

In spreads where cards are arranged in a straight line (like 3-card or 5-card readings), directional energy typically flows from left to right:

Chronological Flow

- The natural left-to-right reading direction suggests temporal progression
- This creates inherent causal relationships where earlier cards influence later ones
- The linear arrangement naturally emphasizes developmental sequences

Reversed Reading

- Reading from right to left reveals underlying causes of current situations
- This reverse chronology shows what preceded and led to present circumstances
- The backward flow illuminates origins and roots rather than outcomes and futures

Zigzag Reading

- Alternating between forward and backward reading creates a more complex picture
- This zigzag pattern reveals how past and future continually influence each other
- The alternating direction shows recursive patterns that might otherwise be missed

Cross Spread Directions

In cross spreads, directional energy flows both horizontally and vertically, creating multiple axes of influence:

Vertical Axis

- Energy flows from past (above) to present (center) to future (below)
- This creates a temporal progression showing development over time
- The vertical direction emphasizes how historical factors shape coming developments

Horizontal Axis

- Energy flows from advice (left) through present (center) to obstacle (right)
- This creates a guidance-implementation-challenge sequence
- The horizontal direction shows how guidance encounters resistance in actual application

Diagonal Flows

- Energy can flow diagonally from past to obstacle or from advice to future
- These diagonal directions reveal indirect influences that might otherwise be overlooked
- The cross-connections show how seemingly unrelated factors impact each other

Tips for Exploring Directional Energy in Readings

Flow Mapping

After laying out the spread, use visual cues to mark directional relationships:

- Draw arrows (actual or imaginary) between cards to show causal flow
- Use different colours or styles to distinguish different types of directional relationships
- Create a flow chart that maps complete pathways through multiple cards

This visual mapping helps both reader and inquirer see the dynamic movement of energy through the spread.

Directional Storytelling

Narrate the reading as a journey that follows the directional flow:

- "This begins with... which leads to... which then creates..."
- Emphasize transitional language that highlights causality and sequence
- Use "because," "therefore," and "which results in" to emphasize directional relationships

This narrative approach brings the directional dynamics to life, making their flowing energy more accessible.

Bidirectional Exploration

Intentionally explore both possible directions between significant card pairs:

- "We can see how X leads to Y, but let's also consider how Y might lead to X..."
- Compare and contrast the insights that emerge from each direction
- Identify which directional relationship seems most relevant to the inquirer's situation

This balanced approach ensures a thorough understanding of the complex relationships between cards.

Intervention Questioning

Use directional understanding to identify where the inquirer has agency:

- "This card is leading to this outcome—how might you redirect this energy?"
- "What would happen if you strengthened or weakened this particular link in the chain?"
- "This cycle is recurring—where would be the most effective point to introduce change?"

This empowering technique helps inquirers see where they can influence directional flows rather than being passively carried by them.

Conclusion: The Dynamic Flow of Oracle Energies

Directional energy in Gypsy Oracle readings reveals the flowing currents that animate the cards, transforming static symbols into living pathways of meaning. By recognizing how cards influence each other through causal connections, transformational sequences, developmental stages, cyclical patterns, and conditional relationships, readers access a dimension of interpretation that brings the reading to life.

This dynamic approach recognizes that the cards tell stories rather than simply stating facts—stories with beginnings, middles, and endings; stories with causes and effects; stories with transformations and cycles. Like following the course of a river from mountain spring to ocean, tracing these directional energies allows us to see not just isolated moments but complete journeys of experience.

By developing sensitivity to these flowing patterns, readers can offer insights that honour life's inherent movement—the way circumstances evolve, transform, and circle back upon themselves in meaningful ways. The cards become not frozen snapshots but flowing narratives whose interweaving currents illuminate both origins and destinations, both established patterns and potential new directions.

This perspective reminds us that life itself is never static—it flows continuously through cycles of beginning and ending, growth and decay, separation and connection. Through understanding directional energy, readers can help inquirers recognize the natural momentum of their circumstances, the causal patterns shaping their experience, and the potential turning points where conscious choice might redirect the flow toward more fulfilling channels.

Practice Techniques for Mastering Directional Energy

Directional Analysis Process

1. Identify Primary Directional Flows
   Begin by noting clear causal or sequential relationships between cards:
   - Which cards seem to naturally flow into others?
   - Where do cause-effect relationships appear most evident?
   - What developmental sequences emerge across multiple cards?
2. Explore Alternative Directions
   Consider how relationships change when the flow is reversed:
   - How does the meaning shift when direction is flipped?
   - Which direction seems most relevant to the inquirer's situation?
   - What insights emerge from considering both possibilities?

3. Map Complete Pathways

    Trace directional flows that connect three or more cards:

    - What stories emerge when following these extended pathways?
    - How does energy transform as it moves through multiple cards?
    - Where do cycles or feedback loops appear?

4. Analyze Conditional Factors

    Note how certain cards create conditions that affect others:

    - Which cards serve as determining factors for others?
    - How do specific cards change the manifestation of others?
    - What if-then relationships are most significant?

5. Identify Intervention Points

    Look for places where directional flow might be redirected:

    - Where could the inquirer influence the directional energy?
    - Which points in causal chains offer opportunity for change?
    - How might cyclical patterns be transformed into progressive ones?

CHAPTER 4

Interpreting Reversed Cards

Understanding Card Reversals

In the Sibilla della Zingara, reversals provide a critical dimension to the reading process, offering nuanced insights that may not be accessible through upright cards alone. When a card appears upside-down in a spread, it invites us to explore deeper, potentially hidden aspects of the archetypal energy it represents.

Unlike systems where reversals simply signify the opposite of a card's upright meaning, in Gypsy Oracle Cards, reversals represent a sophisticated modification of the card's energy—creating space for examining blocked potentials, unconscious influences, internalized expressions, or developmental challenges.

I've included a summary of all the reversed card meanings in Tables 1-6 in the Quick Reference section

Approaches to Reading Reversed Cards

1. **Internalized Expression**

When a card appears reversed, its energy may be directed inward rather than manifesting externally. This suggests that the qualities of the card are being experienced internally or privately, rather than being expressed outwardly in the inquirer's life.

Examples:

- A reversed **Doctor** might indicate self-healing or introspective diagnosis rather than seeking external help
- A reversed **Scholar** could suggest private study or internal processing of knowledge rather than formal education
- A reversed **Joyfulness** might point to quiet, personal happiness rather than outward celebration

2. **Blocked or Obstructed Energy**

Reversals may indicate that the card's energy is present but unable to flow freely, suggesting obstacles, resistance, or difficulties in expressing or accessing this energy.

Examples:

- A reversed **Fortune** suggests luck or opportunity that cannot be fully accessed or utilized
- A reversed **Journey** might indicate travel plans delayed or progress impeded by obstacles

- A reversed **Love** could point to affection that is blocked from full expression or reciprocation

3. Shadow Aspects

Some of the most insightful interpretations of reversals involve exploring the shadow side or less conscious aspects of the archetype. This approach reveals hidden motivations, unconscious patterns, or challenging expressions of the card's energy.

Examples:

- A reversed **Merchant** might reveal exploitative tendencies or purely transactional approaches to relationships
- A reversed **Priest** could indicate spiritual hypocrisy or misuse of moral authority
- A reversed **Friend** might point to codependency or friendship masking ulterior motives

4. Developmental Challenges

Reversals can highlight areas requiring growth, attention, or healing—pointing to qualities or potentials that are underdeveloped or in need of conscious cultivation.

Examples:

- A reversed **Child** suggests challenges with new beginnings or innocence that has been compromised

- A reversed **Constancy** might indicate difficulties with commitment or dependability
- A reversed **Hope** could point to a need to rebuild faith or optimism after disappointment

5. Compensatory Behaviour

Sometimes reversals indicate that the energy of the card is being expressed in compensatory or exaggerated ways, often to mask insecurity or vulnerability in that area.

Examples:

- A reversed **Haughtiness** might suggest arrogance masking deep insecurity
- A reversed **Soldier** could indicate aggressive behaviour compensating for feelings of vulnerability
- A reversed **Lord** might point to authoritarian behaviour stemming from fear of losing control

Specific Card Category Reversals

Relationship Cards

When relationship cards appear reversed, they frequently point to connections that are imbalanced, inauthentic, or operating with hidden dynamics that require attention.

Key Questions for Reversed Relationship Cards:

- What unconscious patterns might be affecting this relationship? Is there an imbalance of power or reciprocity in this connection?

- How might the authentic expression of this relationship be blocked or distorted?
- What shadow aspects of this relational dynamic need to be acknowledged?

Emotion Cards

Reversed emotion cards often point to feelings that are repressed, denied, or expressing in unhealthy ways. They can indicate emotional complexes that require conscious attention and integration.

Key Questions for Reversed Emotion Cards:

- Is this emotion being suppressed or denied?
- How might this feeling be expressing itself indirectly or unconsciously?
- What deeper emotional patterns might be at play beneath the surface?
- Is there emotional work needed in this area?

Occupation Cards

When occupation cards appear reversed, they often suggest professional skills or authorities that are being misused, underdeveloped, or operating in covert ways.

Key Questions for Reversed Occupation Cards:

- How might this professional archetype be operating unconsciously or behind the scenes?

- Is there a misuse or corruption of this occupation's expertise or authority?
- How might the shadow aspects of this professional role be manifesting?
- Is there a need to develop or integrate this professional energy more fully?

Events Cards

When event cards appear reversed, they frequently suggest delayed, interrupted, or internally experienced transitions. They may point to incomplete processes or events unfolding in unexpected ways.

Key Questions for Reversed Event Cards:

- How is this event or transition being delayed or obstructed?
- What aspects of this experience are happening internally rather than externally?
- Is there unfinished business from a past event that needs completion?
- How might resistance to this event be creating complications?

Places and Things Cards

Reversed places and things cards often indicate environments or objects that are not fulfilling their intended purpose, or whose influence is operating in subtle, hidden ways.

Key Questions for Reversed Places and Things Cards:

- How might this environment or object be working in unexpected or contradictory ways?
- What limitations or restrictions are present in this space or with this item?
- Is there a mismatch between the appearance and reality of this place or thing?
- What hidden aspects of this environment or object need to be addressed?

States of Being Cards

Reversed states of being cards often suggest persistent conditions that are either internalized, unstable, or expressing in paradoxical ways that create tension or dissonance.

Key Questions for Reversed States of Being Cards:

- How might this persistent state be operating beneath the surface?
- Is there instability or inconsistency in maintaining this condition?
- What internal contradictions exist within this state?
- How might this mode of being be expressing in compensatory or exaggerated ways?

Reading Methodology with Reversals

Proportion Analysis

The proportion of upright to reversed cards in a reading provides valuable insight:

Mostly Upright: Suggests situations that are largely conscious and externally manifesting

Mostly Reversed: Indicates circumstances with significant unconscious factors or internal processing

Balanced Mix: Points to a situation with both conscious and unconscious elements requiring integration

Progressive Development

Sequences of cards moving from reversed to upright (or vice versa) often tell a story of development:

Reversed to Upright: Suggests evolution from unconscious to conscious, or from internal to external expression

Upright to Reversed: May indicate a process moving from external manifestation to internal integration

Patterns and Groupings

Clusters of reversed cards in specific positions or categories reveal important themes:

Reversed Cards in Future Positions: Often indicate upcoming internal work or challenges requiring conscious attention

Reversed Cards in Past Positions: May suggest unprocessed experiences or unresolved influences

Reversed Cards Grouped by Category: Reveals thematic areas requiring deeper exploration

Deciding Whether to Use Reversals

The decision to incorporate reversals is personal and depends on your reading style, the depth of insight sought, and the specific context of each reading. Some factors to consider when deciding whether or not to use reversals include:

Advantages of Incorporating Reversals:

- Reversals add complexity and nuance to readings
- They provide access to shadow material and unconscious patterns
- They offer a way to explore blocked or internalized energies
- They create a fuller spectrum of interpretative possibilities

Arguments Against Using Reversals:

- They can potentially overcomplicate readings for beginners
- Some readers prefer to derive similar insights through card combinations and positions
- Upright-only readings may be more accessible for inquirers unfamiliar with card reading

- Certain spreads or questions may not benefit from the additional complexity

Developing Your Approach

Many experienced readers find that their relationship with reversals evolves over time. You might begin with upright-only readings while developing familiarity with the cards. As you gain more experience, you can gradually introduce reversals for specific questions. You could start by using reversals for simple spreads (e.g. three card spread) until you feel comfortable using them in every reading.

Experiment with different approaches to decide if using reversals is a method that delivers the most meaningful insights for you. Don't be afraid to develop your own personal system for when and how to incorporate reversals in your readings.

Conclusion

In my experience, using reversals is a powerful way to gain deeper insights into the full spectrum of Gypsy Oracle Card meanings. Reversed cards offer more than a contradiction of upright meanings; they unveil hidden dimensions, developmental roadblocks, and internal projections. By developing sensitivity to the subtle shifts in energy that reversals represent, readers can access profound insights that might otherwise remain veiled, creating readings that honour the full complexity of human experience and the rich wisdom contained within the Gypsy Oracle tradition.

Practice Techniques for Mastering Reversal Interpretation

The Appendix contains an Essential Meanings Quick Reference with reversed meanings for each of the Gypsy Oracle Cards. For more detailed information, see my book, Gypsy Oracle Cards: A Handbook for Interpreting the Sibilla della Zingara.

Journaling Exercise

1. Pull a card upright and spend 5 minutes writing about its standard meaning
2. Turn the same card upside down and spend another 5 minutes exploring how its energy shifts
3. Consider what aspects emerge in reversal that might be hidden in the upright position

Comparative Analysis

1. Conduct two readings on the same question—one with reversals and one without

2. Note the differences in depth, nuance, and insight between the two approaches
3. Reflect on which aspects of the situation each method illuminates

CHAPTER 5

Illustrative Cross Spread Interpretations

The cross spread is one of the most common and versatile layouts used in Gypsy Oracle card readings. This five-card spread provides insight into the past influences, current situation, future developments, challenges, and guidance related to a specific question.

Cross Spread Positions:

- **Center**: The current situation or core issue
- **Above**: Past influences affecting the situation
- **Below**: Future trends or developments
- **Right**: Obstacles or challenges
- **Left**: Advice or guidance

Readers may choose to use a simple cross spread consisting of five cards, one in each position. For more complex questions, it may be necessary to add additional layers to the spread for additional insight.

The following sections contain examples that demonstrate how to interpret the cross spread across various life situations, applying the principles of card combinations, reversals, and directional energy. Each example includes cards in both upright and reversed positions to show how reversals add depth and nuance to the reading.

Simple Cross Spread Interpretation

1. Career Advancement

Question: "What are my prospects for promotion at my current job?"

Center: Merchant (R)
Above: Scholar
Below: Fortune
Right: Constancy (R)
Left: Journey

ILLUSTRATIVE CROSS SPREAD INTERPRETATIONS

Interpretation:

Merchant Reversed at the center suggests your career situation involves challenges with strategic exchanges or business acumen. This reversal indicates you may be struggling with value recognition, fair negotiations, or could be taking a too-transactional approach to your career. Perhaps your contributions aren't being properly valued, or you're having difficulty effectively demonstrating your worth to superiors.

Scholar in the past position shows that your educational background, acquired knowledge, and intellectual preparation have built a strong foundation for your current professional position. Your dedication to learning and developing expertise has significantly contributed to where you stand today.

Fortune in the future position is particularly positive, suggesting unexpected luck and favourable circumstances ahead for your career. This indicates that promotion prospects are indeed promising, with opportunities that may exceed your expectations.

The obstacle position reveals **Constancy Reversed**, suggesting that inconsistency or difficulty with maintaining steady progress may be your biggest challenge. Perhaps you struggle with following through on projects or demonstrating the reliability your superiors are looking for. This reversed card warns that wavering commitment could undermine your advancement.

For advice, **Journey** recommends embracing movement, change, and possibly even physical relocation may be beneficial. This could mean being open to lateral moves within the company, taking on projects that require travel, or considering positions in different departments or locations. The willingness to step beyond your comfort zone appears crucial to your professional advancement.

The combination of **Scholar + Merchant Reversed** reveals how your intellectual foundation hasn't yet translated into proper recognition or exchange value. Meanwhile, **Merchant Reversed + Fortune** suggests that despite current challenges with receiving proper recognition, unexpected opportunities are approaching that will shift this dynamic favourably.

The double reversal pattern of **Merchant Reversed** at center and **Constancy Reversed** as obstacle indicates that both your value expression and your consistency are areas requiring attention. The upright **Journey** as advice offers a pathway out of these reversed energies through embracing new directions and movement.

Direct Answer: Your prospects for promotion are favourable in the longer term, especially if you make some changes in your approach. While you currently face challenges with recognition and consistency, the Fortune card in your future position suggests unexpected opportunities will arise. Rather than staying in your current role waiting for recognition, consider exploring new paths within the company, demonstrating your flexibility and willingness to grow. This movement and adaptation, rather than rigid expectations about how advancement should occur, will likely lead to the promotion opportunities you seek.

2. Finding Love

Question: "Will I meet someone special soon and what can I do to prepare?"

Center: Young Woman)
Above: Room (R)
Below: Love
Right: Frivolity (R)
Left: Service

Interpretation:

Young Woman at the center indicates emerging feminine energy, potential, and development at the heart of your situation. This suggests you're in a period of growth and possibility, with feminine qualities of receptivity and openness being particularly important.

Room Reversed in the past position suggests a history of either insufficient privacy or perhaps an inner world turned upside down—confusion, disorder, or lack of boundaries. This reversal indicates you may have struggled to maintain personal space or clear perspective, perhaps overexposing yourself or having unclear boundaries in previous relationships.

Love in the future position is extremely favourable for your question, indicating genuine romantic connection and passion are indeed approaching. This card directly answers your question with a positive affirmation that meaningful romantic connection is on the horizon.

The obstacle position shows **Frivolity Reversed**, which actually has a positive implication—it suggests that a period of superficiality or irresponsible approach to relationships is ending. Perhaps you're moving beyond casual encounters or no longer approaching love with a lighthearted detachment. This reversal shows growth away from immature relationship patterns.

For advice, **Service** recommends cultivating a helpful, attentive, and supportive attitude. This suggests preparing for love by developing your capacity to care for others and attend to their needs rather than focusing solely on what you hope to receive.

ILLUSTRATIVE CROSS SPREAD INTERPRETATIONS

The progression from **Room Reversed** through **Young Woman** to **Love** tells a developmental story: from disordered personal boundaries through emerging self-development to genuine romantic connection. The reversed Room as past influence suggests that creating healthier internal space has been a necessary part of your journey toward love.

The combination of **Frivolity Reversed** as obstacle with **Service** as advice creates a powerful complementary energy—you're naturally moving away from superficiality (Frivolity Reversed) and the advice to develop your capacity for care (Service) reinforces this maturation process. This alignment between your natural evolution and the recommended approach suggests particularly favourable conditions for meaningful relationship development.

Direct Answer: Yes, you will meet someone special relatively soon, as indicated by the Love card in your future position. The cards suggest you're already on the right path, moving away from superficial connections toward something more meaningful. To prepare, focus on developing your capacity to be attentive and supportive to others—genuine service rather than self-focused expectations will create the right foundation for the meaningful relationship that's approaching. Creating clearer personal boundaries and continuing your current path of growth and maturation will naturally attract the deep connection you're seeking.

3. Relationship Assessment

Question: "Is my current relationship healthy and heading toward commitment?"

Center: Wedding
Above: Love (R)
Below: House
Right: Falseness (R)
Left: Conversation

Interpretation:

Wedding at the center places formal commitment and partnership at the heart of your question, directly addressing your concerns about the relationship's future.

Love Reversed in the past position suggests that the relationship may have begun with challenges in emotional connection—perhaps unrequited feelings, love that wasn't fully expressed, or emotional incompatibility. This reversal indicates that despite current movement toward commitment, the emotional foundation may have had initial struggles or imbalances.

House in the future position is extremely favourable, suggesting stability, security, and creating a home together. This points to a relationship that is indeed moving toward greater permanence and shared foundation-building.

The obstacle position reveals **Falseness Reversed**, which has a positive implication—it suggests that deception or insincerity that may have been present is ending or being revealed. Perhaps past miscommunications or unspoken truths are being addressed, clearing the way forward.

For advice, **Conversation** emphasizes the crucial importance of open dialogue, clear communication, and meaningful exchange. This suggests that honest communication is the key to navigating the path toward the commitment you're considering.

The transformation from **Love Reversed** through **Wedding** to **House** shows a remarkable healing journey—moving from emotional challenges or imbalances through formal commitment to creating stable partnership. This progression suggests that whatever difficulties existed in the emotional foundation are being transformed through commitment into something stable and secure.

The combination of **Love Reversed** in the past with **Falseness Reversed** as obstacle reveals a powerful pattern of healing—both emotional disconnection and inauthenticity are being overcome. The **Conversation** advice works directly with both of these reversed energies, as open dialogue helps heal both emotional distance and lack of transparency.

Direct Answer: Yes, your relationship is healing and heading toward deeper commitment. While there may have been emotional challenges or imbalances in the beginning (Love Reversed), the relationship is evolving in a positive direction. The presence of Wedding in the center and House in the future position strongly indicates movement toward formal commitment and creating a stable home together. What makes this particularly healthy is that past issues of insincerity or miscommunication are being resolved (Falseness Reversed). To support this positive trajectory, maintain open and honest dialogue about both your feelings and expectations—the Conversation card suggests this transparency is crucial for the relationship to fulfil its potential for lasting commitment.

ILLUSTRATIVE CROSS SPREAD INTERPRETATIONS

4. Health Concern

Question: "What can I do to improve my chronic fatigue and overall wellbeing?"

Center: Malady
Above: Merchant (R)
Below: Doctor (R)
Right: Constancy
Left: Journey

Interpretation:

Malady at the center confirms that your question centers on illness, weakness, or imbalance, directly reflecting your health concerns about chronic fatigue.

Merchant Reversed in the past position suggests problematic exchanges or exploitative relationships may have contributed to your current condition. This reversal indicates you may have been giving more than receiving, engaging in unfair trades of your energy or health, or perhaps making poor investments with your physical resources. There's a suggestion of imbalanced transactions that have depleted rather than sustained you.

Doctor Reversed in the future position is cautionary, suggesting potential challenges with finding effective healing solutions or properly diagnosing your condition. This reversal warns of possible misdiagnosis, ineffective treatments, or healthcare professionals who may not fully understand your condition. It calls for careful discernment in your healing journey and perhaps seeking multiple opinions or approaches.

The obstacle position shows **Constancy**, which interestingly suggests that consistency itself may be partially problematic. Perhaps rigid routines or an unwillingness to change established patterns is impeding your recovery. Alternatively, this could indicate that the persistent nature of your condition is the primary challenge.

For advice, **Journey** recommends embracing movement, change, and possibly literal travel or relocation. This suggests that physical movement, changing environments, or completely altering your approach to health may be beneficial. This could range from trying new treatment modalities to considering significant lifestyle changes.

The combination of **Merchant Reversed** in past and **Doctor Reversed** in future creates a challenging pattern around exchanges—unfair trades of energy in the past connect to potential ineffective exchanges in healthcare contexts in the future. This suggests being particularly mindful about who you entrust with your healing and what you give of yourself in the process.

The contradiction between **Constancy** as obstacle and **Journey** as advice highlights a key tension in your recovery: the need to break from established patterns and embrace change rather than maintaining current approaches. This opposition is particularly significant given the reversals elsewhere in the spread, suggesting that transformation of your approach is essential for healing.

Direct Answer: To improve your chronic fatigue and overall wellbeing, the cards suggest you need to fundamentally change your approach rather than continuing with established patterns. The Journey card specifically recommends embracing movement, change, and possibly new environments. This could include exploring alternative healing modalities, changing your physical space, incorporating more varied movement into your routine, or even travelling for healing purposes. Be cautious about healthcare providers who may not fully understand your condition (Doctor Reversed) and seek multiple perspectives. Also, examine how you've been investing your energy in the past—the Merchant Reversed suggests you've been giving more than receiving in important exchanges. Breaking consistent patterns (Constancy as obstacle) and creating new, more variable rhythms that honour your energy levels may be key to your recovery.

5. Financial Decision

Question: "Should I invest my savings in the property I'm considering?"

Center: Money (R)
Above: Thought
Below: House
Right: Thief
Left: Scholar (R)

Interpretation:

Money Reversed at the center suggests you may be experiencing financial anxiety, scarcity consciousness, or challenges with resource management. This reversal indicates your relationship with this potential investment may be coloured by financial insecurity or fear of loss rather than a clear-headed assessment of value.

ILLUSTRATIVE CROSS SPREAD INTERPRETATIONS

Thought in the past position indicates that careful consideration, analysis, and reflection have preceded this potential investment. This suggests you've been appropriately thoughtful in your approach to this financial decision.

House in the future position creates a direct connection to property investment, suggesting that real estate or home-related investments may indeed be favourable. This alignment between your question about property and the House card appearing in the future position is particularly significant.

The obstacle position reveals **Thief**, warning of potential loss, exploitation, or hidden costs. This suggests being extremely cautious about the specific property or investment terms, as there may be risks of financial loss or being taken advantage of in some way.

For advice, **Scholar Reversed** cautions against overthinking or getting lost in endless research without action. This reversal suggests you may be using intellectual analysis as a way to avoid making a decision, or perhaps missing practical considerations while focusing on theoretical knowledge. It warns against analysis paralysis and recommends balancing research with intuition and practical common sense.

The progression from **Thought** through **Money Reversed** to **House** shows a challenging pathway—moving from intellectual consideration through financial anxiety to potential property acquisition. The reversed Money in the center suggests this transition may be more emotionally difficult than financially problematic.

The combination of **Money Reversed** at center and **Thief** as obstacle creates a particularly challenging energy around financial security and potential loss. Meanwhile, **Scholar Reversed** as advice suggests that more research may not actually help—you might already have sufficient information but are struggling with the emotional aspects of the decision rather than lacking facts.

Direct Answer: The cards present a cautious "yes" regarding this property investment, but with important qualifications. While the House card in the future position suggests the property investment could eventually provide stability, significant risks exist that require careful assessment. You should be particularly vigilant about hidden costs or potentially exploitative terms (Thief). More research (Scholar Reversed) is unlikely to resolve your concerns, as your hesitation appears more emotional than factual. Your financial anxiety (Money Reversed) may be colouring your perspective, making it difficult to evaluate objectively. If you decide to proceed, have all terms thoroughly reviewed by professionals, negotiate aggressively to protect yourself from potential exploitation, and be prepared for some initial financial stress before the investment stabilizes.

ILLUSTRATIVE CROSS SPREAD INTERPRETATIONS

6. Major Life Transition

Question: "I'm considering relocating to another country for work. Is this the right move for me?"

Center: Journey (R)
Above: Prison
Below: Fortune
Right: House (R)
Left: Faithfulness

Interpretation:

Journey Reversed at the center indicates blocked movement, frustrated progress, or resistance to necessary transition. This reversal suggests you may be experiencing internal resistance to the relocation, delays in the process, or uncertainty about this major life change. The energy of movement is present but obstructed or complicated.

Prison in the past position suggests you've been experiencing confinement, restriction, or limitation in your current situation. This indicates that your desire to relocate may be driven by feeling trapped or constrained in your present circumstances.

Fortune in the future position is extremely favourable, suggesting that if you overcome the current blockages, this move will likely bring unexpected luck, opportunities, and positive outcomes. This strongly supports the relocation being beneficial for you, despite current hesitations or obstacles.

The obstacle position shows **House Reversed**, indicating challenges related to establishing stability, finding appropriate housing, or creating a sense of home in the new location. This suggests potential difficulties with the practical aspects of settling in a new country, including possible housing insecurity or difficulty feeling "at home" initially.

For advice, **Faithfulness** recommends maintaining loyalty, consistency, and trustworthiness through this transition. This suggests honouring commitments, maintaining important relationships, and staying true to your core values even as external circumstances change dramatically.

The transformation from **Prison** through **Journey Reversed** to **Fortune** shows a powerful potential progression—moving from constraint through a challenging transition period to unexpected opportunity. This sequence suggests that working through the current resistance or delays is worthwhile, as fortunate circumstances await on the other side.

The double reversal pattern of **Journey Reversed** at center and **House Reversed** as obstacle indicates that both the movement itself and the establishment of a new home space are challenging aspects of this relocation. The upright **Faithfulness** as advice offers a stabilizing anchor amid these reversals—maintaining inner consistency can provide the necessary foundation during external transitions.

Direct Answer: Yes, relocating to another country for work is ultimately the right move for you, though it won't be without challenges. The Fortune card in your future position indicates that unexpected opportunities and positive outcomes await you if you make this transition. Your current situation (Prison in past position) is restrictive and limiting, making change necessary for your growth. However, the process won't be smooth—you're experiencing internal resistance or external delays (Journey Reversed), and establishing a stable living situation initially may be difficult (House Reversed). To navigate these challenges successfully, maintain your core values and commitments throughout the transition (Faithfulness). Staying true to yourself while embracing change will help you move through the difficult adjustment period to reach the fortunate circumstances that await you abroad.

7. Educational Path

Question: "Should I pursue the advanced degree I'm considering, or focus on gaining practical experience?"

Center: Scholar (R)
Above: Child
Below: Merchant
Right: Waiting (R)
Left: Journey

Interpretation:

Scholar Reversed at the center suggests challenges with intellectual pursuits or academic approaches—perhaps overthinking, intellectual arrogance, or knowledge that remains theoretical rather than practical. This reversal indicates you may be questioning the value of formal education or experiencing doubts about academic pathways.

Illustrative Cross Spread Interpretations

Child in the past position indicates that your educational journey began with innocent curiosity, openness to learning, and fresh potential. This suggests your academic interests stem from genuine enthusiasm and natural intellectual inclination.

Merchant in the future position suggests that your educational path will ultimately lead to practical application, strategic exchange, and potentially financial reward. This indicates that whichever path you choose will eventually connect to professional opportunity and practical value.

The obstacle position reveals **Waiting Reversed**, which suggests impatience with processes that take time, difficulty with delayed gratification, or frustration with necessary periods of anticipation. This reversal indicates you may be struggling with the extended timeline required for formal education, wanting faster results or more immediate application.

For advice, **Journey** recommends embracing exploration, movement, and varied experiences. This suggests that your educational development might benefit from diverse learning environments and practical applications rather than solely academic pursuit.

The progression from **Child** through **Scholar Reversed** to **Merchant** suggests a challenging but ultimately rewarding path—moving from innocent curiosity through questioned academic approaches to practical application and exchange value. The reversal in the middle of this sequence suggests that formal education alone may not be the most direct path to your goals.

The combination of **Scholar Reversed** at center and **Waiting Reversed** as obstacle reveals a significant tension around academic timelines—frustration with both theoretical knowledge and the time required to acquire it. The **Journey** advice works directly with both of these reversed energies, suggesting that movement, varied experience, and exploration may be more aligned with your current learning needs than traditional academic pathways.

Direct Answer: Based on the cards, focusing primarily on practical experience rather than pursuing an advanced degree seems better aligned with your current needs and temperament. The Scholar Reversed in the center position suggests formal academic study may lead to overthinking or knowledge that remains theoretical rather than practical. Your impatience with extended timelines (Waiting Reversed) would make the lengthy commitment of an advanced degree particularly challenging. However, the Journey card as advice suggests a third option might be ideal—a learning path that combines practical experience with education in a more flexible, exploratory way. This could include certificate programs, workshops, mentorships, or project-based learning that provides credentials while allowing immediate application. The Merchant in your future indicates that whatever educational path you choose will ultimately lead to practical value and financial reward, but the direct academic route may not be the most efficient path for you right now.

Illustrative Cross Spread Interpretations

8. Family Conflict

Question: "How can I heal the ongoing conflict with my sibling that has divided our family?"

Center: Foe (R)
Above: Haughtiness
Below: Reunion
Right: Falseness
Left: Consolation (R)

Interpretation:

Foe Reversed at the center suggests that hostile energies are diminishing or that enemies may be becoming allies. This reversal suggests the conflict may be softening, oppositions becoming less intense, or a gradual shift toward potential reconciliation. While challenges remain, there's an indication that the purely adversarial relationship is evolving toward something more nuanced.

Haughtiness in the past position suggests that pride, excessive self-importance, or arrogance has contributed significantly to the current conflict. This indicates that wounded ego, perception of superiority, or inability to show humility may have initiated or escalated the division.

Reunion in the future position is extremely favourable, suggesting that reconciliation, coming together, and healing of the relationship is indeed possible. This provides hope that the family division can be overcome.

The obstacle position reveals **Falseness**, indicating that deception, insincerity, or misleading appearances continue to impede resolution. This suggests that unspoken truths, pretense, or lack of authenticity is maintaining the conflict.

For advice, **Consolation Reversed** cautions that comfort might be missing or ineffective in its current form. This reversal suggests that standard approaches to providing emotional support may be insufficient or even counterproductive. Perhaps sympathy without truth, or comfort that avoids addressing core issues, is prolonging rather than healing the conflict.

The transformation from **Haughtiness** through **Foe Reversed** to **Reunion** shows a powerful healing journey—moving from pride through diminishing conflict to eventual reconciliation. This progression suggests that while the process of healing has begun with softening opposition (**Foe Reversed**), it requires addressing deeper issues to reach genuine reunion.

Illustrative Cross Spread Interpretations

The combination of **Falseness** as obstacle with **Consolation Reversed** as advice reveals a challenging dynamic—superficial or insincere comforting (**Consolation Reversed**) cannot overcome deception (**Falseness**). This suggests that resolution requires moving beyond platitudes or easy sympathy to more authentic, if initially uncomfortable, truth-telling that addresses the real issues at the heart of the conflict.

Direct Answer: To heal the ongoing conflict with your sibling, you need to address the underlying inauthenticity in your interactions rather than offering superficial comfort. The cards suggest the conflict is already naturally diminishing (Foe Reversed) and reconciliation is possible (Reunion), but pretense and lack of genuine communication (Falseness) remain significant obstacles. Standard approaches to emotional support won't be effective (Consolation Reversed)—in fact, attempting to comfort without addressing core issues may be prolonging the conflict. The path to healing requires acknowledging how past pride or ego (Haughtiness) contributed to the division, then engaging in honest, potentially uncomfortable conversations that address the real issues rather than maintaining polite facades. This truthful approach, though initially more difficult than offering simple sympathy, will create genuine resolution and the family reunion indicated in your future position.

9. Creative Block

Question: "How can I overcome my artistic block and reconnect with my creative inspiration?"

Center: Waiting
Above: Scholar (R)
Below: Child
Right: Prison (R)
Left: Frivolity

Interpretation:

Waiting at the center indicates that your creative situation is characterized by anticipation, expectancy, and suspended action—the essence of a creative block where you're waiting for inspiration to return.

Illustrative Cross Spread Interpretations

Scholar Reversed in the past position suggests that intellectual arrogance, overthinking, or misuse of knowledge may have contributed to your current block. This reversal indicates that overanalysis, rigid thinking patterns, or perhaps an overemphasis on technique at the expense of intuition has stifled your natural creative flow.

Child in the future position is extremely favourable for creative renewal, suggesting a return to innocence, fresh beginnings, and untainted potential. This indicates that reconnecting with playful, uninhibited creative expression is indeed possible.

The obstacle position reveals **Prison Reversed**, which actually has a positive implication—it suggests that constraints are lifting, limitations are easing, or a period of confinement is ending. This reversal indicates that while you perceive yourself as blocked, you may already be in the process of becoming free from the restrictions that have limited your creativity.

For advice, **Frivolity** recommends embracing playfulness, spontaneity, and carefree experimentation. This suggests that lighthearted exploration without concern for outcomes or judgments may be the key to breaking your creative block.

The progression from **Scholar Reversed** through **Waiting** to **Child** tells a transformative story—moving from overintellectualization through a necessary pause to rediscovered creative innocence. This sequence offers hope that your current block is actually part of a natural creative evolution.

The combination of **Prison Reversed** as obstacle with **Frivolity** as advice creates a powerful complementary energy—you're naturally moving out of confinement (**Prison Reversed**) and the recommendation to embrace play (**Frivolity**) accelerates this process. This alignment between your natural evolution and the recommended approach suggests particularly favourable conditions for creative renewal.

Direct Answer: To overcome your artistic block and reconnect with creative inspiration, embrace playfulness and spontaneity rather than continuing to overthink your creative process. The cards suggest your block stemmed from over-intellectualizing your art (Scholar Reversed), but the constraints are already naturally lifting (Prison Reversed). The Child card in your future position indicates you're on a path toward renewed creative innocence and fresh beginnings. The most effective approach now is to deliberately engage with Frivolity—experiment without concern for outcomes, play with your medium without judgment, and approach creative work with a lighthearted spirit rather than heavy seriousness. This playful approach will accelerate your natural movement away from confinement and help you reconnect with the childlike wonder and spontaneity that fuels authentic creativity. The Waiting at the center suggests patience is also needed—trust that this period of suspended creativity is part of a natural cycle leading toward renewal.

ILLUSTRATIVE CROSS SPREAD INTERPRETATIONS

10. Spiritual Guidance

Question: "I feel disconnected from my spiritual path. How can I deepen my practice and reconnect with my sense of purpose?"

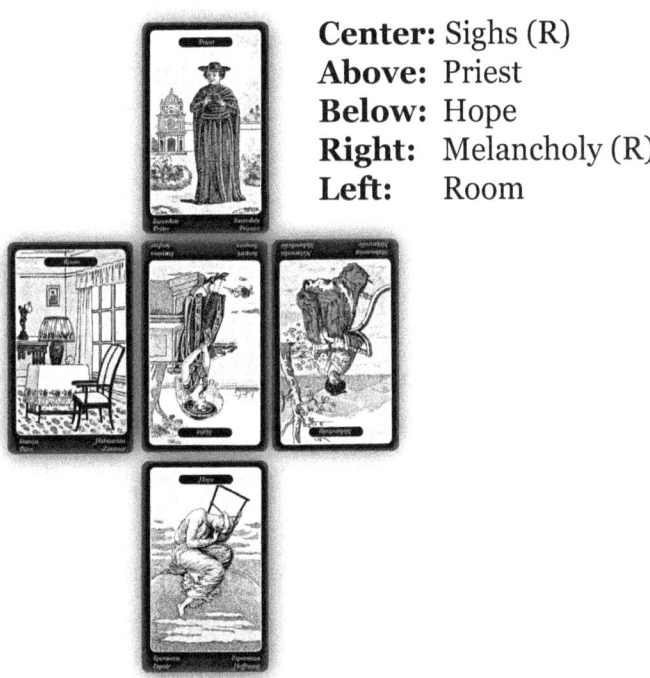

Center: Sighs (R)
Above: Priest
Below: Hope
Right: Melancholy (R)
Left: Room

Interpretation:

Sighs Reversed at the center suggests that the period of yearning, longing, or unfulfilled spiritual desire may be ending. This reversal indicates that while you perceive yourself as disconnected, you may actually be at a turning point where the feelings of separation are beginning to lift. What appears as disconnection might actually be transition.

Priest in the past position suggests that your previous spiritual approach may have been more formal, traditional, or focused on external authority and moral frameworks. This indicates that your spiritual foundation contains elements of established wisdom or structured practice.

Hope in the future position is favourable, suggesting that renewed optimism, inner vision, and faith in positive outcomes is developing. This indicates that reconnection with spiritual purpose and meaning is indeed possible and emerging.

The obstacle position shows **Melancholy Reversed**, which suggests you're moving beyond reflective sadness or introspective grief that may have been part of your spiritual journey. This reversal indicates that excessive rumination or dwelling on spiritual disappointments is lifting, clearing the way for renewed connection.

For advice, **Room** recommends creating private space, inner sanctuary, and time for intimate contemplation. This suggests that your spiritual renewal requires deliberate creation of sacred space and boundaries that protect your inner work.

The transformation from **Priest** through **Sighs Reversed** to **Hope** shows a powerful spiritual journey—moving from formal or external spiritual practice through a turning point in spiritual seeking to renewed personal faith and vision. This progression suggests you're already in tran-

Illustrative Cross Spread Interpretations

sition from longing to hope, even if you don't fully recognize it yet.

The combination of **Melancholy Reversed** as obstacle with **Room** as advice creates an insightful pairing—as you naturally move beyond spiritual sadness (**Melancholy Reversed**), creating intentional space for contemplation (**Room**) will accelerate this healing process. The advice to create sacred space works in harmony with the natural lifting of spiritual heaviness that is already occurring.

Direct Answer: To deepen your spiritual practice and reconnect with your sense of purpose, create dedicated sacred space for personal contemplation. The cards suggest you're actually at a turning point (Sighs Reversed) where your feeling of disconnection is already beginning to shift toward renewed hope and vision. You're naturally moving beyond past spiritual disappointments (Melancholy Reversed), and this process will accelerate if you intentionally create boundaries that protect your inner work (Room). This may represent a shift from more traditional, externally-focused spiritual practice (Priest) toward a more personal, direct experience. Unlike your past approaches which may have relied more on external authority or structure, this new phase requires creating your own sacred space—both literally and figuratively—where authentic connection can flourish. By honouring this transition with intentional time for contemplation, you'll discover that what felt like disconnection was actually the beginning of a deeper, more personally meaningful spiritual path.

Multi-layer Cross Spread Interpretation

Question: Is my current venture going to be successful?

Spread:

Center: Lord (reversed), Messenger, Waiting (reversed), Malady

Above: Joyfulness (reversed), Journey, Foe, Surprise

Below: Letter, Servant, Love, Room

Left: Reunion (reversed), Child, Sorrow, Thought (reversed)

Right: Prison, Haughtiness, Soldier (reversed), Hope

Illustrative Cross Spread Interpretations

Interpretation:

Center Position (Current Situation):

Lord (reversed), Messenger, Waiting (reversed), Malady

The center of your spread reveals the core energy of your venture. The reversed Lord suggests challenges with authority or leadership - perhaps you're struggling with confidence in directing this venture or there may be issues with how authority is being exercised. The Messenger brings communication and news, indicating information exchange is central to this venture. Waiting reversed suggests impatience or a situation where things are moving faster than anticipated, perhaps prematurely. Malady points to weakness or vulnerability at the core of the situation.

Together, these cards suggest a venture characterized by communication challenges, leadership issues, hasty movement, and underlying vulnerabilities. This core shows a project that has potential but faces significant foundational challenges.

Above Position (Past/Influences):

Joyfulness (reversed), Journey, Foe, Surprise

The past influences show that what began with diminished joy or happiness (Joyfulness reversed) led to movement and change (Journey). The Foe indicates competition or opposition that has influenced your path, while Surprise suggests unexpected developments that have shaped your direction.

This position reveals that your venture emerged from a period of reduced happiness, prompting you to embark on a new path. You've faced opposition and unexpected turns that have brought you to this point.

Below Position (Future):

Letter, Servant, Love, Room

Your future path shows communication (Letter) combined with supportive service (Servant), genuine affection or passion for the work (Love), and private space for development (Room).

This is the most positive position in your spread, suggesting that the future holds productive communication, helpful support, genuine passion, and the necessary space for your venture to develop. These cards indicate that despite current challenges, there is potential for the venture to find its footing.

Left Position (Advice):

Reunion (reversed), Child, Sorrow, Thought (reversed)

The advice position suggests that reconciliation with past connections may not be helpful (Reunion reversed). Instead, embracing new beginnings with openness (Child) is recommended. The presence of Sorrow indicates you must be willing to process grief or disappointment along the way. Thought reversed warns against overthinking or analysis paralysis.

This position advises a fresh approach rather than trying to revive past methods, willingness to experience and process setbacks, and action rather than excessive contemplation.

Right Position (Obstacles):

Prison, Haughtiness, Soldier (reversed), Hope

Your obstacles include restrictive circumstances (Prison) and excessive pride or arrogance (Haughtiness) - perhaps your own or within your venture's culture. Soldier reversed suggests lack of discipline or protection, while Hope indicates that optimism might paradoxically be an obstacle - perhaps creating unrealistic expectations.

These obstacles point to constraints, ego issues, lack of structure, and potentially misplaced optimism that could interfere with your venture's success.

Card Combinations and Patterns

Looking at the patterns across positions:

> **Amplification of Communication Themes**: Messenger in center with Letter in future suggests that communication will become increasingly important as your venture develops.

Transformation from Opposition to Support: Moving from Foe in past to Servant in future indicates a shift from facing obstacles to receiving assistance.

Balance Needed Between Restriction and Freedom: Prison as obstacle with Room in future shows the challenge of moving from constraint to having appropriate space for growth.

Directional Energy from Impatience to Development: Waiting reversed in center flowing toward the Room in future suggests that current haste needs to evolve into measured, private development.

Answer to Your Question

Based on this cross spread, your current venture shows potential for success, but success is not guaranteed in its current form. The spread indicates that:

- The venture currently faces significant leadership and structural challenges
- Past opposition and unexpected developments have shaped its course
- Future success depends on effective communication, supportive relationships, and genuine passion
- To succeed, you'll need to embrace new approaches, process disappointments, and take action rather than overthinking
- Obstacles including restrictions, ego issues, and lack of discipline need to be addressed

The most promising aspect is the future position, suggesting that with the right adjustments, your venture can evolve toward success. However, the challenging center position indicates that the current approach may need significant modification.

Your venture appears to be in a transitional state - with potential for success if you can address the core issues indicated in the center position, follow the advice of embracing new approaches, and overcome the obstacles of restriction and lack of discipline.

For greatest chance of success, focus on strengthening leadership, ensuring proper structure, cultivating supportive relationships, and creating appropriate space for your venture to develop organically at its own pace.

Final thoughts on Cross Spread Interpretation

These interpretations demonstrate how the cross spread with reversed cards can provide particularly nuanced insights across diverse life situations. Reversals add important dimensions of internalized expression, blocked energy, shadow aspects, developmental challenges, and compensatory behaviours that might not be visible through upright cards alone. By analyzing the relationships between upright and reversed cards—their combinations, contradictions, transformations, balances, proximities, and directional energies—readers can offer powerful guidance that honours the full complexity of human experience.

It's important to note that while the interpretations presented here are grounded in the traditional meanings of the cards, these same card combinations could yield different insights depending on the reader. Every practitioner must ultimately rely on their own intuitive gifts when interpreting a spread. The card meanings provide a foundation and framework, but intuition serves as the bridge that connects these archetypal energies to the inquirer's specific circumstances.

The most powerful readings emerge when readers balance knowledge of traditional meanings with their intuitive response to the cards in the context of the specific question and the inquirer's situation. This balance allows the rich wisdom contained within the Gypsy Oracle tradition to be applied with both precision and personal relevance, creating interpretations that resonate deeply with the inquirer's lived experience.

As you develop your practice with the cross spread, remember that your unique perspective and intuitive insights are valuable additions to the traditional meanings. Trust both your knowledge and your intuition as complementary tools that together create readings of exceptional depth and utility.

Quick Reference Guides

Upright and Reversed Card Meanings

Table 1: Relationship Cards

Card	Upright	Reversed
Child	Pregnancy, baby, birth, childhood, new project or relationship, fresh start, creativity, naivety	Failed pregnancy plans, failed plans, immature venture / not going forward, indecisiveness, imprudent actions
Enemy	Male rival, opposition, confrontation, espionage, distrust, impostor, unexpected conflict, unaware of problem	End of argument/hostility/obstacle, deception was a joke, close call, danger detected
Foe	Female rival, competition, fake friend, wickedness, hypocrisy, bad advice, intrigues, self-inflicted barriers	Danger imminent, love rival or dangerous person already doing damage, dispute removed or avoided
Friend	Friendship, trust, security, faithfulness, help, attentiveness, good advice, positive news	Unfaithful friend, someone who can't keep secrets, misunderstanding, argument, isolation

Card	Upright	Reversed
Lord	Protection, guidance, advice, gentleman, employer, boss, nobility, wealth, status, educated	Man of poor character, selfish employer, irresponsible professional, fallen man, deception
Lover	Boyfriend, husband, lover, devotion, adoration, loyalty, acknowledgment of self-worth	Immature love, unfaithful, unrequited love, uncertainty, confusion, doubts, questioning feelings, removal of beloved
Old Woman	Mother, grandmother, aunt, female professor, mature woman, fortune teller, reassuring, good advice, wisdom	Woman not supportive, bad advice, meddling, interference, situation stuck in past
Servant	Professional, faithful, respectful, household staff, secretaries, support staff, caring	Betrayal of trust, taking advantage, unproductive/lazy, unable to accept help
Sweetheart	Girlfriend, wife, lover, bride, devotion, generosity, sensuality	Unrequited love, disappointment, heartbreak, time to move on, rival no longer in picture
Widower	Person living with loneliness/sadness/loss/abandonment, mourning, regrets, need to accept situation	End of solitude and sadness, time to move on, or sudden irreparable ending

Quick Reference Guides

Card	Upright	Reversed
Wife	Trustworthy, loyal, honest, caring, supportive, maternal, steadfast, committed relationship	Break, separation, divorce, person not faithful, neglects responsibilities, frivolous
Young Woman	Damsel, daughter, sister, cousin, young lover, sweet, reliable, maturing, growing, developing	Lack of maturity, frivolity, something small and insignificant, listless, frail, lazy

Table 2: Emotion Cards

Card	Upright	Reversed
Cheerfulness	Celebration of achievement or life event, social gatherings, good mood affecting all aspects of life, time to celebrate / enjoy yourself	Denied job, failed exam, unsuccessful pregnancy, wedding interrupted, broken engagement, illness or death
Despair	Jealousy, unreasonable thoughts, feeling disgraced/betrayed/humiliated, shame, fear, scandal	Interrupted moment of despair, jealousy present but not yet causing despair, end to reckless behaviour
Faithfulness	Loyalty, support from friends/family/colleagues, protection, good omen, positive results, trust your instincts	Infidelity, disloyalty, betrayal, misplaced trust, breach of duty, ignored responsibility
Falseness	Betrayal, deception, lies, corruption, defensiveness, fake or two-faced person, trying to cover up a mistake	Truth coming out, secrets revealed, deceptions uncovered, insincere behaviours ceasing
Haughtiness	Arrogance, conceit, vanity, showing off, overly ambitious, excess of pride	Healthy awareness of limitations and strengths, need to be more confident, restored relationships

Quick Reference Guides

Card	Upright	Reversed
Hope	Anticipation, believing in positive outcome, clairvoyance, psychic powers, confidence in favourable resolution	Disrupted plans for future, misplaced hopes, dampened enthusiasm, pessimism, discontent
Joyfulness	Glee, gaiety, pleasure from entertainment, satisfaction, relief, resolution, achievements, promotions	Disappointment, restlessness, lack of ideas/initiative/peace, anxiety, goals not achieved
Love	New love, happy in love, affection, intense feelings, romance, sensuality	End of love, love not mutual, volatility, frustration, falling out of love, lost attraction
Melancholy	Dwelling on mistakes/disappointments, abandonment, depression, upset, grief, anguish, anxiety, regrets	Emotional breakdown, love gone wrong, unhappy family situation, loss of friendship/job/money
Sorrow	Profound sadness, anguish, pain, grief, separation, broken heart, money or health problems	Pain and sorrow ending, madness, "sky is falling" feeling, or magnification of sorrow with negative cards
Surprise	Better than expected outcome, unexpected money/reward/win/bonus, surprise visit/letter/phone call, good news, lucky break	Hope not realized, postponed positive outcome, luck not on your side, delayed or sub-optimal outcome

Table 3: Occupation Cards

Card	Upright	Reversed
Doctor	Medicine man/woman, trusted advisor, need for emotional/physical healing, stress	Person of no help, unprepared or unwilling to take advice, closed-minded, refusing help
Merchant	Financial gain, profitable investments, professional, successful businessman, good decisions	Business failure, warning against investing/new venture/negotiation, defeat, financial difficulties
Messenger	Official communication, announcement, results, invitation, letter, phone call, email	Message or information not coming, lazy/ineffective messenger, message delayed
Pleasure Seekers	Exuberance, spirited, situation out of control, group of friends, peer pressure, recklessness, going along with the crowd	Behaviour leading nowhere, errors in judgment, state of confusion, defeat due to unwise behaviour, blindly following
Priest	Spirituality, morality, beliefs, ecclesiastic person, confessor, legal opinions, regulations, conventional approach	Loss of morality, injustice, prejudice, errors in judgment, immoral individual

Quick Reference Guides

Card	Upright	Reversed
Scholar	Expert, connoisseur, wise councillor, professor, researcher, guidance, wisdom, experience, intellect, accurate information	Lack of preparation/study, failure of examination, lack of consideration, nonsense
Soldier	Military, officer, young professional, on guard against hostility, protection, justice	Lack of protection/help, untrustworthy person, jealous, possessive, controlling, confining
Thief	Sudden unexpected loss, someone who cheats/steals/meddles, deception, betrayal, deceit, carelessness resulting in loss	Dishonest actions continue to have effect, falsification of documents, misplaced confidence, close call but nothing lost

Table 4: Events Cards

Card	Upright	Reversed
Death	Ending, divorce, time to move on, sudden change, upheaval, metamorphosis, transition, rebirth	Situation very negative, significant upheaval, physical death, end of feeling/job/business
Fortune	Lucky streak, dreams come true, victorious, happy at work, positive business transactions, change for better	Luck not on your side, need for prudent action, slowdown, betrayal, loss of game, rejection
Journey	Trip, vacation, relocation, moving, agility, evolution, change, going forward, making progress	Failed trip, cancelled vacation, journey to avoid, missed appointment, lack of momentum, blocked progress
Conversation	Dialogue, discussion, communication, exchange of information, clarification, apologies, being heard	Lack of clarification, lack of communication, postponed conversations, things unsaid, silence is golden
Misfortune	Disgrace, fall from grace, accident, mishap, sudden/unexpected/unpredicted negative event	Irreparable loss with finality, painful event destroying hopes, or end of misfortune (with positive cards)
Malady	Illness, weakened state, disease, inability to cope, burdened, unpleasant changes	Healing, end of confusion/sickness/hindrance, resolution of issues

Card	Upright	Reversed
Reunion	Reunion, reconnection, meeting, appointment, invitation, clarification, resolution, fresh start, satisfactory solution	Missed/postponed appointment, meeting avoided, failure to resolve, no reconciliation
Wedding	Important event, ceremony, new responsibilities, contracts, unions, loss of independence	Something fate won't unite, unrequited/impossible love, cancelled wedding, broken engagement / partnership

Table 5: Places and Things Cards

Card	Upright	Reversed
House	Family and emotional bonds, home, office, security, responsibilities, self-reliance, independence	Breakdowns in family relationships, quarrels, misunderstandings, broken dreams, divorce, loss of security, homeless
Gift	Winnings, inheritance, abundance, improved situation, successful endeavour, achievement	Loss, gift not received, lost inheritance, financial loss or debt, inability to save money
Letter	Message, document, answer, approval, contract, new opportunity or challenge	Message or document not coming or late, loved one not writing, confirmation not arriving
Money	Earned income, savings, winnings, luck, success and prosperity within reach, responsible budgets, confidence, self-worth	Loss of money, gambling losses, money wasted, complications from inadequate funding, irresponsible with money
Prison	Confined, restrained because of past choices, difficulty moving on, shame, guilt, self-punishment, anxiety, regret, remorse, exile, loneliness	End of punishment, release from confining circumstance, lifting of restraints
Room	Intimacy, privacy, receiving guests, being welcomed, need to retreat or reflect, something/someone missing	World turned upside down, inner turmoil, confusion, loss of perspective, impulsive behaviour

Table 6: States of Being Cards

Card	Upright	Reversed
Consolation	Realization of desires, satisfaction, esteem, well-being, unexpected opportunity or results, future holds favourable period / positive changes / approval / honours	Missed or wasted opportunities, failure to receive expected comfort or relief, unexpected disappointment, what's coming is not a positive outcome
Constancy	Continuity, steadiness, reliability, steadfast, consistency, solidity, purposeful, patient, long term	Inconsistency, hesitation, impulsive behaviour, lack of stability, unfair or unreliable person
Frivolity	Undecided, fickle, irregular, impulsive, thoughtless, superficial	End of superficial behaviour, end of carefree time, inability to maintain commitments, perilous behaviour
Service	Receiving help or offering help, well-mannered, respectful, dutiful, helpful staff, paid work	Help not arriving, enemy disguised as friend, undermining efforts, rival, two-faced person, someone working against you

Card	Upright	Reversed
Sighs	Searching for answer/solution, anticipation, expectation, isolation, abandonment, loneliness, difficulty letting go, regrets over loss	End of waiting for something desired, desired person has returned, wish granted, or no hope
Thought	Contemplation, introversion, reflection, indecision, planning, decision making, judgment, research, study	Lack of thought/consideration/reflection, thoughtless, impulsive, troubled mind, worry
Waiting	Waiting for someone/event/answers, yearning, hoping, wishing, anticipation, arrival of person/news	Waiting unnecessarily, disillusionment, pointless to wait, person will not come, rejection

Energetic Categorization of Gypsy Oracle Cards

This categorization is based on the traditional interpretations, but it's important to note that many cards can shift meaning based on context, surrounding cards, and whether they appear upright or reversed.

Table 7: Positive Cards

Cheerfulness	A joyful card symbolizing celebration and positive social events
Child	A positive card indicating new beginnings and creative potential
Consolation	A very positive card predicting recovery and unexpected opportunity
Constancy	A positive card representing steadfastness and reliability
Faithfulness	A positive card symbolizing loyalty and trust
Fortune	A very positive card indicating luck and unexpected prosperity
Friend	A positive card representing trustworthy support and good cheer
Gift	Generally a good omen suggesting unexpected blessings
Hope	A positive card providing encouragement for the future
House	A positive card symbolizing security and stability
Joyfulness	A very positive card signifying genuine happiness
Love	A positive card representing deep emotional connection
Lover	A positive card representing devotion and ideal partnership

Lord	A positive card symbolizing noble protection and guidance
Money	A positive card symbolizing abundance and resources
Reunion	A positive card indicating reconnection and reconciliation
Service	A positive card suggesting help and support
Surprise	A positive card representing unexpected joy or favourable events
Sweetheart	A positive card representing devotion and love
Waiting	A positive card symbolizing anticipation with eventual positive outcome
Wedding	A positive card representing formal commitment and partnership
Wife	A positive card representing trustworthiness and support
Young Woman	A positive card representing sweetness and potential

Table 8: Negative Cards

Death	A negative card signifying definitive endings
Despair	A negative card revealing destructive emotions
Enemy	A negative card warning of opposition and betrayal
Falseness	A negative card suggesting deception and insincerity
Foe	A negative card representing someone interfering in your life
Malady	A negative card representing suffering or weakness
Melancholy	A card representing sadness and regret
Misfortune	A negative card symbolizing catastrophic setbacks
Prison	A negative card symbolizing confinement and limitation
Sorrow	A negative card symbolizing acute grief and loss
Thief	A negative card suggesting sudden unexpected loss
Widower	A negative card representing loneliness and mourning

Table 9: Neutral Cards

Conversation –	A neutral card representing dialogue
Doctor	Generally positive card representing advice
Frivolity	Generally positive but warns of superficiality
Haughtiness	Can be positive when balanced, negative when excessive
Letter	Neutral card signifying important communication
Merchant	Primarily positive but can suggest materialism
Messenger	Usually considered positive but depends on the message
Old Woman	A positive card but neutral in influence
Pleasure Seekers	Can be positive or negative depending on context
Priest	A neutral card symbolizing judgment and morality
Room	A neutral card representing private space
Scholar	A neutral card representing wisdom and knowledge
Servant	Positive but with warnings about motivations
Sighs	Represents yearning that can be positive or negative
Soldier	Influenced by situation and associated cards
Thought	A neutral card representing reflection and analysis
Journey	Primarily positive but can indicate departures

QUICK REFERENCE GUIDES

Table 10: Amplification Combinations

The following table presents powerful card combinations that illustrate the principle of amplification in Gypsy Oracle readings. These pairings reveal how cards can enhance each other across various life themes, from love and personal growth to challenges and transformations. By recognizing these amplified combinations, readers can offer more nuanced insights into the intensified energies shaping an inquirer's situation.

Theme	Combination	Amplified Effect
Exceptional Love	Fortune + Love	Divinely blessed romantic connection with extraordinary harmony
Passionate Devotion	Lover + Sweetheart	Intensely mutual romantic adoration with exceptional depth
Unwavering Loyalty	Friend + Faithfulness	Exceptionally reliable and steadfast supportive connections
Stable Partnership	Wedding + House	Particularly enduring union with strong foundations
Profound Healing	Doctor + Scholar	Exceptionally effective healing through combined expertise and understanding
Reliable Support	Constancy + Service	Extraordinarily dependable assistance that never wavers
Resilient Positivity	Hope + Joyfulness	Remarkably persistent optimism and authentic happiness
Fortunate Beginnings	Child + Surprise	Exceptionally promising new starts arriving unexpectedly
Abundant Prosperity	Fortune + Money	Extraordinary financial luck leading to exceptional wealth

Theme	Combination	Amplified Effect
Profitable Exchange	Merchant + Gift	Particularly advantageous business opportunities or deals
Protected Security	Lord + House	Exceptionally stable foundation with powerful protection
Financial Recovery	Money + Reunion	Particularly meaningful restoration of prosperity or resources
Devastating Loss	Misfortune + Thief	Exceptionally severe pattern of losses affecting multiple areas
Determined Opposition	Enemy + Foe	Particularly intense hostility from multiple sources
Painful Betrayal	Falseness + Despair	Exceptionally distressing deception causing deep emotional wounds
Confined Grief	Prison + Sorrow	Particularly restrictive circumstances with acute emotional pain
Final Separation	Death + Widower	Exceptionally definitive ending with profound mourning
Catastrophic Ending	Misfortune + Death	Particularly devastating conclusion requiring complete rebuild
Cunning Exploitation	Thief + Falseness	Exceptionally deceptive manipulation leading to significant loss
Deep Emotional Pain	Sorrow + Sighs	Particularly intense grief combined with persistent yearning
Compound Difficulty	Malady + Melancholy	Exceptionally challenging state affecting body and spirit

Quick Reference Guides

Theme	Combination	Amplified Effect
Prideful Restriction	Prison + Haughtiness	Particularly difficult confinement made worse by excessive pride
Careless Insincerity	Frivolity + Falseness	Exceptionally superficial deception lacking both depth and authenticity
Anxious Anticipation	Despair + Waiting	Particularly difficult emotional state during period of anticipation
Resilient Optimism	Misfortune + Hope	Exceptionally powerful faith maintained despite devastating circumstances
Insightful Restriction	Prison + Thought	Particularly profound understanding gained through limitation
Transformative Renewal	Death + Child	Exceptionally powerful rebirth following complete ending
Enduring Through Pain	Sorrow + Constancy	Particularly steadfast persistence despite emotional distress
Exploratory Stability	Journey + House	Exceptionally meaningful movement that reinforces foundations
Playful Wisdom	Scholar + Frivolity	Particularly effective learning combining depth and lightheartedness
Rewarded Patience	Waiting + Fortune	Exceptionally fortunate outcomes following period of anticipation

Theme	Combination	Amplified Effect
Supportive Authority	Lord + Servant	Particularly effective leadership combining direction and assistance
Hopeful Recovery	Malady + Consolation	Exceptionally effective healing through timely comfort
Transformative Communication	Conversation + Reunion	Particularly powerful reconciliation through open dialogue
Jealous Control	Despair + Soldier	Exceptionally restrictive behaviour driven by intense fear of loss
Superficial Success	Frivolity + Fortune	Particularly lucky outcomes despite careless approach
Wise Protection	Scholar + Soldier	Exceptionally effective defence through strategic understanding
Generous Prosperity	Gift + Money	Particularly abundant resources shared with exceptional generosity
Liberating Knowledge	Scholar + Journey	Exceptionally expansive learning through varied exploration
Deceptive Loss	Falseness + Death	Particularly devastating ending based on fundamental dishonesty

Quick Reference Guides

Table 11: Transformation Combinations

The following table presents card combinations that illustrate the principle of transformation in Gypsy Oracle readings.

Transformation Theme	Card Combination	Transformative Process
Complete Renewal	Death + Child	Total ending creates space for entirely fresh beginning unburdened by the past
Fortune from Disaster	Misfortune + Fortune	Catastrophe disrupts patterns, paradoxically creating openings for unexpected blessings
From Grief to Love	Widower + Lover	Complete mourning process eventually enables capacity for new romantic connection
Sorrow into Joy	Sorrow + Joyfulness	Acute grief transmutes into more profound capacity for authentic happiness
Liberating Movement	Prison + Journey	Limitations trigger impulse for exploration, finding freedom through movement
From Enemy to Ally	Enemy + Friend	Opposition develops qualities that eventually create mutual connection and respect
Insincerity to Truth	Falseness + Constancy	Experiencing deception catalyzes commitment to unwavering authenticity
Pride to Service	Haughtiness + Service	Isolation of arrogance triggers recognition of the value of supportive connection

Transformation Theme	Card Combination	Transformative Process
Loss as Medicine	Thief + Doctor	What is taken provides crucial insights that enable deeper healing and wholeness
Weakness to Comfort	Malady + Consolation	Vulnerability becomes means through which timely support is attracted
Despair to Optimism	Despair + Hope	Depths of jealousy and negativity catalyze extraordinary resilience and vision
Sadness to Blessing	Melancholy + Gift	Introspective grief creates receptivity to unexpected opportunities
Lightness to Depth	Frivolity + Thought	Limitations of superficiality trigger desire for deeper contemplation
Deception to Wisdom	Falseness + Scholar	Disorientation of being misled becomes impetus for committed learning
Potential to Wisdom	Young Woman + Old Woman	Journey of development transforms possibility into embodied knowledge
Dialogue to Insight	Conversation + Thought	Exchange with others catalyzes profound personal reflection
Conflict to Resolution	Foe + Reunion	Rivalry creates tension that eventually resolves into reconciliation
Waiting to Receiving	Waiting + Gift	Patient anticipation creates receptivity for unexpected offering

Quick Reference Guides

Transformation Theme	Card Combination	Transformative Process
Sighs to Fulfilment	Sighs + Fortune	Wistful yearning attracts the very opportunities longed for
Isolation to Connection	Room + Reunion	Private introspection prepares ground for meaningful reconnection
Jealousy to Love	Despair + Love	Intense attachment fear transforms into secure affectionate connection
Theft to Abundance	Thief + Money	Experience of loss creates value recognition leading to greater prosperity
Confusion to Clarity	Pleasure Seekers + Scholar	Chaotic experience triggers desire for ordered understanding
Rigidity to Flow	Soldier + Journey	Disciplined structure creates foundation for expansive exploration
Loss to Recovery	Misfortune + Doctor	Devastating setback catalyzes profound healing process
Judgment to Compassion	Priest + Consolation	Moral evaluation transforms into supportive understanding
Division to Unity	Foe + Wedding	Opposition creates tension that resolves into formal partnership
Superficiality to Reliability	Frivolity + Constancy	Carefree inconsistency triggers desire for dependable commitment

Transformation Theme	Card Combination	Transformative Process
Deception to Liberation	Falseness + Journey	Discovering dishonesty catalyzes movement toward authentic freedom
Longing to Comfort	Sighs + Consolation	Wistful yearning attracts the very comfort being sought
Illness to Strength	Malady + Constancy	Temporary weakness develops into enduring resilience
Fear to Protection	Despair + Soldier	Jealous insecurity transforms into structured boundaries
Isolation to Service	Room + Service	Private reflection creates foundation for helpful contribution
Doubt to Faith	Melancholy + Faithfulness	Thoughtful sadness transforms into unwavering loyalty
Restriction to Prosperity	Prison + Money	Limitation creates focused discipline leading to resource development
Opposition to Insight	Enemy + Scholar	Adversarial experience catalyzes deeper understanding
Grief to Guidance	Widower + Old Woman	Mourning process transforms into mature wisdom
Surprise to Stability	Surprise + House	Unexpected development creates foundation for security
Theft to Gift	Thief + Gift	Taking without permission transforms into generous offering

Quick Reference Guides

Transformation Theme	Card Combination	Transformative Process
Superficial to Sacred	Frivolity + Priest	Light-hearted play evolves into reverence for deeper principles

Table 12: Contradicting Card Combinations

The following table presents card combinations that illustrate the principle of contradicting card in Gypsy Oracle readings.

Card	Contradicting Card	Nature of Contradiction
Cheerfulness	Melancholy	Joy versus sadness; celebration versus introspection
Child	Old Woman	Innocence versus wisdom; beginning versus maturity
Consolation	Sorrow	Relief versus grief; comfort versus pain
Constancy	Frivolity	Steadfastness versus carefree attitude; reliability versus inconsistency
Death	Child	Endings versus beginnings; completion versus new potential
Despair	Hope	Overwhelming negativity versus optimistic expectation
Enemy	Friend	Opposition versus support; threat versus alliance
Faithfulness	Falseness	Loyalty versus deception; sincerity versus insincerity
Foe	Friend	Rivalry versus alliance; competition versus cooperation
Fortune	Misfortune	Unexpected luck versus unexpected setback; prosperity versus loss
Gift	Thief	Receiving versus losing; generosity versus taking
Haughtiness	Servant	Pride versus humility; self-importance versus service to others

Card	Contra-dicting Card	Nature of Contradiction
Hope	Despair	Optimism versus overwhelming negativity; faith versus fear
House	Journey	Stability versus movement; rootedness versus exploration
Joyfulness	Sorrow	Heartfelt happiness versus acute grief; celebration versus mourning
Lord	Servant	Authority versus service; leadership versus support
Love	Despair	Deep connection versus isolation; affection versus jealousy
Lover	Widower	Devotion versus loss; connection versus separation
Malady	Doctor	Illness versus healing; weakness versus restoration
Melancholy	Cheerfulness	Reflective sadness versus exuberant joy; introspection versus celebration
Merchant	Thief	Fair exchange versus unjust taking; commerce versus theft
Misfortune	Fortune	Disaster versus luck; setback versus advancement
Old Woman	Child	Wisdom versus innocence; experience versus potential
Pleasure Seekers	Thought	Indulgence versus reflection; group exuberance versus individual contemplation
Priest	Falseness	Moral authority versus deception; spiritual truth versus lies

Card	Contradicting Card	Nature of Contradiction
Prison	Journey	Confinement versus freedom; restriction versus movement
Reunion	Death	Coming together versus final separation; reconciliation versus ending
Room	Journey	Private space versus movement; interiority versus exploration
Scholar	Frivolity	Deep study versus light-heartedness; analysis versus play
Service	Haughtiness	Helpfulness versus self-importance; support versus ego
Sighs	Joyfulness	Yearning versus fulfilment; wistfulness versus celebration
Soldier	Pleasure Seekers	Discipline versus indulgence; order versus revelry
Sorrow	Consolation	Acute grief versus comfort; pain versus relief
Surprise	Constancy	Unexpected development versus steady continuity; sudden change versus reliability
Sweetheart	Widower	Romantic devotion versus mourning love; connection versus loss
Thief	Gift	Taking versus giving; exploitation versus generosity
Thought	Pleasure Seekers	Reflection versus indulgence; analysis versus emotional expression
Waiting	Journey	Anticipation versus movement; patience versus action

Card	Contra-dicting Card	Nature of Contradiction
Wedding	Widower	Union versus separation; commitment versus loss
Wife	Falseness	Trustworthiness versus deception; reliability versus insincerity
Young Woman	Old Woman	Development versus maturity; growth versus wisdom

Table 13: Comprehensive Progression Sequences

This table lists examples of progression sequences and the narrative suggested by the progression.

Theme	Progression Sequence	Developmental Narrative
Relationship Formation	Friend + Conversation + Lover + Wedding	From friendship and dialogue to romance and commitment
Relationship Healing	Falseness + Sorrow + Conversation + Reunion	From deception and pain through dialogue to reconciliation
Relationship Dissolution	Frivolity + Falseness + Despair + Death	From superficiality through deception to jealousy and ending
Family Formation	Wedding + Love + Child + House	From commitment to affection to new life and stability
Career Development	Scholar + Merchant + Lord + Fortune	From learning through strategic exchange to leadership and success
Career Setback	Thief + Foe + Misfortune + Death	From loss through opposition to disaster and ending
Healing Journey	Malady + Doctor + Consolation + Joyfulness	From illness through treatment to comfort and happiness
Emotional Recovery	Sorrow + Melancholy + Waiting + Hope	From acute grief through reflection to patience and optimism

Quick Reference Guides

Theme	Progression Sequence	Developmental Narrative
Creative Process	Thought + Conversation + Service + Gift	From idea through dialogue to implementation and offering
Spiritual Growth	Frivolity + Prison + Thought + Priest	From superficiality through limitation to reflection and wisdom
Financial Progress	Service + Merchant + Money + Fortune	From work through exchange to resources and prosperity
Financial Loss	Falseness + Thief + Misfortune + Sighs	From deception through theft to disaster and longing
Learning Process	Child + Young Woman + Scholar + Old Woman	From innocence through development to knowledge and wisdom
Transformational Crisis	Misfortune + Prison + Death + Child	From disaster through confinement to ending and rebirth
Journey of Self-Discovery	Journey + Thought + Constancy + Service	From exploration through reflection to reliability and contribution
Rising from Adversity	Sorrow + Consolation + Hope + Fortune	From grief through comfort to optimism and good fortune
Falling from Grace	Haughtiness + Falseness + Foe + Misfortune	From pride through deception to opposition and downfall
Artistic Development	Frivolity + Thought + Scholar + Gift	From playfulness through reflection to mastery and creation

Theme	Progression Sequence	Developmental Narrative
Disillusionment	Hope + Waiting + Sighs + Melancholy	From optimism through anticipation to yearning and sadness
Restoration of Trust	Falseness + Prison + Thought + Faithfulness	From deception through limitation to reflection and loyalty
Leadership Journey	Young Woman + Scholar + Doctor + Lord	From potential through knowledge to expertise and authority
Romantic Disenchantment	Lover + Conversation + Melancholy + Death	From passion through dialogue to sadness and ending
Practical Mastery	Scholar + Thought + Doctor + Service	From knowledge through reflection to expertise and application
Personal Liberation	Prison + Thought + Death + Journey	From confinement through reflection to ending and movement
Social Integration	Room + Conversation + Friend + Pleasure Seekers	From privacy through dialogue to friendship and celebration
Professional Advancement	Service + Lord + Money + House	From support through authority to prosperity and stability
Character Development	Frivolity + Falseness + Prison + Constancy	From lightness through deception to restriction and reliability
Wisdom Acquisition	Child + Room + Scholar + Old Woman	From innocence through privacy to knowledge and wisdom

Theme	Progression Sequence	Developmental Narrative
Communal Building	Friend + Conversation + Wedding + House	From alliance through dialogue to commitment and stability
Material Success	Service + Gift + Money + Fortune	From work through opportunity to resources and luck

Table 14: Comprehensive Balance Combinations

This table provides examples of balance combinations and suggested tension interpretations.

Balance Theme	Card Combination	Equilibrium Dynamic
Reliability & Spontaneity	Constancy + Frivolity	Steadfast dedication balanced with light-hearted spontaneity
Discipline & Joy	Soldier + Pleasure Seekers	Ordered precision balanced with joyful celebration
Stability & Movement	House + Journey	Grounded security balanced with expansive exploration
Authority & Service	Lord + Servant	Decisive command balanced with humble supportiveness
Intellect & Passion	Scholar + Lover	Thoughtful analysis balanced with heartfelt devotion
Analysis & Emotion	Thought + Joyfulness	Deep contemplation balanced with genuine happiness
Principle & Connection	Priest + Friend	Ethical discernment balanced with warm acceptance
Wisdom & Innocence	Old Woman + Child	Mature insight balanced with innocent curiosity

Quick Reference Guides

Balance Theme	Card Combination	Equilibrium Dynamic
Strategy & Generosity	Merchant + Gift	Shrewd assessment balanced with unearned blessing
Humility & Pride	Service + Haughtiness	Selfless attention balanced with healthy self-respect
Patience & Action	Waiting + Journey	Calm expectancy balanced with forward momentum
Healing & Release	Doctor + Thief	Restorative skill balanced with necessary letting go
Optimism & Depth	Hope + Melancholy	Positive vision balanced with reflective consideration
Opportunity & Limits	Fortune + Prison	Abundant luck balanced with defining boundaries
Trust & Vigilance	Friend + Foe	Supportive connection balanced with cautious assessment
Loyalty & Freshness	Faithfulness + Surprise	Steady dedication balanced with openness to the unexpected
Speaking & Listening	Conversation + Thought	Expressive dialogue balanced with quiet reflection
Security & Vulnerability	Soldier + Child	Protective strength balanced with innocent openness

Balance Theme	Card Combination	Equilibrium Dynamic
Planning & Intuition	Scholar + Surprise	Careful preparation balanced with spontaneous insight
Grief & Renewal	Widower + Young Woman	Respectful mourning balanced with developing potential
Care & Independence	Doctor + Journey	Attentive treatment balanced with autonomous movement
Giving & Receiving	Service + Gift	Deliberate offering balanced with gracious acceptance
Structure & Creativity	House + Child	Established framework balanced with fresh innovation
Doubt & Faith	Melancholy + Faithfulness	Thoughtful questioning balanced with unwavering trust
Solitude & Connection	Room + Conversation	Private reflection balanced with social exchange
Devotion & Freedom	Wedding + Journey	Committed partnership balanced with personal exploration
Analysis & Action	Scholar + Merchant	Thorough research balanced with practical implementation
Caution & Boldness	Thought + Fortune	Careful consideration balanced with fortunate risk-taking

Quick Reference Guides

Balance Theme	Card Combination	Equilibrium Dynamic
Rest & Activity	Room + Pleasure Seekers	Quiet retreat balanced with social engagement
Order & Growth	Soldier + Young Woman	Disciplined structure balanced with developing potential
Critique & Support	Foe + Consolation	Challenging assessment balanced with comforting assistance
Speaking & Silence	Messenger + Room	Active communication balanced with receptive listening
Tradition & Innovation	Old Woman + Surprise	Time-tested wisdom balanced with unexpected novelty
Worldly & Spiritual	Merchant + Priest	Practical commerce balanced with ethical principle
Caution & Trust	Thief + Friend	Protective vigilance balanced with open connection
Loss & Discovery	Widower + Child	Honouring endings balanced with embracing beginnings
Passion & Peace	Lover + House	Intense connection balanced with stable security
Depth & Lightness	Scholar + Frivolity	Serious study balanced with playful approach

Balance Theme	Card Combination	Equilibrium Dynamic
Effort & Grace	Service + Fortune	Deliberate work balanced with effortless blessing
Freedom & Commitment	Journey + Wedding	Independent exploration balanced with formal partnership

About the Author

 From an early age, M. Jacqueline Murray possessed a keen intuitive sensitivity to the energies surrounding people and situations. Born into an Italian heritage that cherishes traditional divination practices, Jacqueline was naturally drawn to the Sibilla della Zingara, or Gypsy Oracle Cards, which became her primary tool for intuitive guidance.

Jacqueline has dedicated herself to mastering the intricacies of this ancient system, developing a uniquely insightful approach to card interpretation that blends traditional wisdom with psychological understanding. Her readings are known for their remarkable accuracy and depth, offering not just predictions but profound insights into the archetypal energies shaping one's circumstances.

Jacqueline is the author of the definitive English language guide to the Sibilla della Zingara, *Gypsy Oracle Cards, A Handbook for Interpreting the Sibilla della Zingara*, bringing these powerful cards to a wider audience and preserving their traditional wisdom while making it accessible to contemporary readers. This groundbreaking work has established her as a leading authority on the Gypsy Oracle tradition outside of its native Italy.

Jacqueline brings a rare combination of analytical precision and intuitive depth to her work with the cards. With advanced degrees in science and business, her background spans environmental science, medical innovation, and strategic marketing; experiences that have honed her ability to translate complex concepts into accessible wisdom. This unique perspective allows her to bridge the worlds of rational analysis and intuitive knowing in her approach to the Gypsy Oracle tradition.

A true global citizen with homes in the USA, Italy, and Canada, Jacqueline's multilingual fluency and extensive travels have exposed her to diverse cultural traditions that enrich her understanding of universal archetypal patterns. When not writing or conducting readings, she pursues photography and music, believing that all creative expressions access the same wellspring of inspiration that informs her card interpretations.

Through this book, Jacqueline shares her comprehensive knowledge of the Sibilla della Zingara, hoping to help others develop their own intuitive relationship with these powerful cards and access the profound wisdom they contain.

For additional resources and reading services, visit Jacqueline's website, where she continues to share her expertise and insights into the fascinating world of the Gypsy Oracle Cards: www.GeoGypsyJacqui.com

Acknowledgments

I was motivated to produce this book by the many wonderful people who have reached out to ask for more information after studying my Gypsy Oracle Cards handbook. Analyzing reviews that readers have left also gave me inspiration, as many asked for more detail on how to interpret the cards beyond their essential meanings.

The Gypsy Oracle Cards I use, and described in this book, are made and distributed by Lo Scarabeo. The Lo Scarabeo brand is known worldwide in the Tarot, divination and New Age circles. In the United States, the brand is known through its partnership with Llewellyn, the largest New Age publisher in the world. The cards are available for purchase through both of their websites, and at numerous retail shops specializing in divination supplies and Amazon. I hope the cards will remain in production for decades to come because I believe they are a powerful tool, unlocking the intuitive powers and igniting creativity and insight of both novice and experienced readers alike.

www.ingramcontent.com/pod-product-compliance
Lightning Source LLC
Chambersburg PA
CBHW050337010526
44119CB00049B/587